THE POEMS OF

ANDREW MARVELL

ANDREW MARVELL

THE POEMS OF
ANDREW MARVELL

Marvell, Andrew

Edited with an Introduction and Commentary

by

JAMES REEVES

and

MARTIN SEYMOUR-SMITH

BARNES & NOBLE, INC.
PUBLISHERS: BOOKSELLERS: SINCE 1873

SBN 389 01018 9

ANDREW MARVELL 1621–1678

INTRODUCTION AND COMMENTARY
© JAMES REEVES & MARTIN SEYMOUR–SMITH 1969
FIRST PUBLISHED 1969

First published in the United States by Barnes & Noble
New York 10003

Printed in Great Britain by Morrison and Gibb Ltd
London and Edinburgh

CONTENTS

v

INTRODUCTION

I

ANDREW MARVELL, poet, private tutor, civil servant, anonymous satirist, pamphleteer and politician, was born on 31 March 1621 at Winestead-in-Holderness, near Hull. His father (also Andrew) was an Anglican parson, of a Cambridgeshire family; his mother, Anne, was a Yorkshirewoman. In 1624 Andrew Marvell, senior, was elected 'Lecturer' of Holy Trinity Church, Hull, and the family moved to the outskirts of Hull. Marvell attended the Grammar School (of which his father was not, as has sometimes been stated, headmaster) there until 1633, when he went up to Trinity College, Cambridge, as the Grammar School's Exhibitioner and a College Scholar.

In 1638 his mother died, and in the same year the Rev. Andrew Marvell married Lucy Alured. In 1641 he was drowned in the Humber. It seems likely that had he lived he would have sided with Parliament in the Civil War.

Marvell was in residence at Trinity for seven years. In 1639 he took his B.A., and became briefly converted to Roman Catholicism. His father is said to have discovered him in a London bookshop and to have persuaded him back into the Anglican faith. Nothing is known of his life at the University.

About the same time as King Charles raised his standard at Nottingham, Marvell left England for a Grand Tour of Holland, Switzerland, France, Italy and Spain; he appears to have acquired a good knowledge of their languages. He was back in London possibly by 1646, but certainly in 1649. At this time his views may be described as moderately Royalist (see the elegy on Lord Hastings, p. 152); but by 1650, when he wrote *An Horatian Ode upon*

I

Cromwell's Return from Ireland, he had decided to go along with the times and became a moderate Parliamentarian. Certainly he abandoned an overtly Royalist position.

Early in 1651 he became tutor in foreign languages to the daughter of Lord Thomas Fairfax of Nunappleton House in his own native Yorkshire. It is likely that in the two years he spent there he wrote the majority of the lyrics for which he is chiefly remembered. Fairfax was a moderate Parliamentarian and an army commander, who had disagreed with the execution of the King and who had consequently retired from his command. He was a typical cultivated, intelligent aristocrat of the political centre, and there is every reason to suppose that he and Marvell agreed on most subjects. Fairfax wrote verse and took a keen interest in literature.

In 1652/3, Marvell's task of teaching Mary Fairfax having come to an end, he emerged into public life. At the same time he seems virtually to have given up writing lyrical poetry. Whether this was the result of a deliberate decision or of a failure of inspiration we have no way of knowing; but at least we can say that with this cessation of poetic activity on the part of Marvell, the tradition of English poetry as it had existed since Chaucer—the tradition that runs through the early Tudor lyristry, Spenser, Ben Jonson and the Cavaliers and the metaphysicals—came to an end. Dryden, younger than Marvell by nine years, inaugurated a tradition that was utterly different in spirit. This is confirmed by the fact that when Marvell's poems were published after his death in 1681, they were purchased for no reason other than that their author had a reputation as a daring anonymous satirist and member of the opposition to King Charles II. In the next century Swift valued highly, and was influenced by, Marvell as a prose satirist, but never mentioned his poems. Interest in these did not evince itself until the Romantic period.

We know from a letter of Milton's to Bradshaw on 21 February 1652/3 that Marvell was then seeking a post with the government. He did not then obtain it, but was appointed tutor to a ward of Cromwell's, William Dutton, who was living in the house of John

Oxenbridge at Eton. In 1657 he became Assistant in the office of the Foreign Secretary, and in 1658 he was elected as one of the two members of Parliament for Hull. Except for a very short period in 1659 he remained an M.P. for the rest of his life.

Marvell, who remained a constitutional monarchist, was nevertheless a vigorous member of the parliamentary opposition, and a daringly outspoken—though necessarily anonymous—satirist. In a licentious age his personal behaviour, like that of Dryden, seems to have been sober; but he was on at least two occasions involved in minor brawls, once in the House of Commons and once while travelling abroad. He enjoyed wine.

From 1663 to 1665 he travelled to Russia, Denmark, Germany and Sweden as Secretary to the Embassy of the Earl of Carlisle. After dinner one night near Hamburg, his waggoner refused to continue the journey unless his friend was allowed to accompany him. Marvell clapped a pistol to his head, and was immediately surrounded by a 'barbarous rout of peasants and Mechanicks'. Luckily the party managed to subdue them and was able to continue. Marvell was away for the better part of two years on this journey.

In 1672 Marvell published the first part of the prose satire *The Rehearsal Transpros'd*, which brought him more fame in his lifetime than any other of his works. Taking its title from the Duke of Buckingham's farce, *The Rehearsal*, it attacked the pretensions of Samuel Parker, who later became Bishop of Oxford. The second part, a reply to attacks on it, followed in 1673. *The Rehearsal Transpros'd* might be summed up as, essentially, a plea for religious toleration. After all, although Marvell was neither a lover of Roman Catholics nor an admirer of the political abilities of the Stuarts, he acknowledged the right of the future James II to change his religion 'for conscience's sake'. This work, like most of the pamphlets he wrote towards the end of his life, emphasizes the necessity of behaving as a Christian as well as of expressing Christian ideas.

Although the 1681 edition of his poems was prefaced by a note signed by 'Mary Marvell', who claimed to be his widow, Marvell did not marry. This Mary Palmer had been Marvell's landlady. A year before his death he was hiding two undischarged bankrupts in a home, in Great Russell Street, which he had taken in the name of Mary Palmer. When he died, on 10 August 1678, the two bankrupts entered into a plot with Mary Palmer to recover £500 of their money which Marvell had deposited, in his own name, with a goldsmith. Owing to her imposture, they eventually succeeded in regaining the money. Marvell's action appears to have been undertaken for the sake of friendship: both the bankrupts came from his own town of Hull. It is ironic that by it he ensured the survival of the work for which he is best known, since Mary Palmer would not otherwise have issued the book.

II

Marvell is among the most enigmatic of all poets. He has been called a revolutionary and a Royalist, a nonconformist and an Anglican; in reality, when he wrote his best poems, he was none of these. He seems to have combined in his personality Puritan high-mindedness with conspicuous pragmatism, intellectual seriousness with playful wit. His earliest poems show him to have been a committed Royalist; later he supported the Cromwellian Settlement; still later he supported—though very critically—the constitutional position of the Stuart monarchy. However, there is a thread of consistency running through his writings. Although he accepted Cromwell as the leader of the nation, he believed that he should accept the crown, as *The First Anniversary* demonstrates. And he always made a very strong distinction between personal and political function. Clearly he was at his happiest when with the retired Fairfax; but that could not go on for ever. It was at Nunappleton that he wrote most of his lyrical poems. True, there is strictly speaking no evidence that he wrote more than three or four of them at the time; but the supposition is nevertheless an irresistible one. There is no hint to the contrary.

4

There has been much discussion about Marvell's political, religious and philosophical views, and some of it is excellent. *Destiny His Choice: The Loyalism of Andrew Marvell*, by John M. Wallace, the most detailed examination of Marvell's political poetry and prose, establishes beyond doubt that he was neither wholly Royalist nor wholly Puritan, and that he was no turncoat. In our notes in this edition, however, we have concentrated as much as possible upon the meaning of the lyrical poems as poems in themselves, and we have consequently emphasized the attitudes of Marvell the poet—complex, subtle, witty, but dedicated above all to expressing the truth as far as his times would allow—rather that of the politician, the theologian or the philosopher.

His poetic beginnings, as demonstrated in *Flecknoe* (p. 66), were in the direction of metaphysical 'wit': parts of this poem, as has been pointed out, are strongly influenced by the Donne of the satires. But in this early poem Marvell had not yet found himself. As a lyrical poet he was always 'metaphysical', and never rejected the influence of Donne; but he developed Donne's style in a manner peculiar to himself. He was always, as George Williamson has observed, 'enamoured with mathematics as a handmaid to metaphysical wit'.

Like all major poets, Marvell was an eclectic in that he saw both sides of fundamental questions. He sought to gather together, into one attitude, the best in all differing views: to combine the best in Anglicanism with the best in Puritanism, the best in Royalism with the best in Republicanism (though he was always a monarchist), the best in sensuousness with the best in spirituality. He was a reconciler of apparent opposites, and his best poems can never be understood if they are read as statements of this or that particular political or philosophical point of view. *Upon Appleton House*, Marvell's longest poem, is, as John M. Wallace has said, 'one of the most eclectic poems of the seventeenth century, a net in which are entangled the impressions of Marvell's wide reading and scholarship'. *Upon Appleton House* is not Marvell's most beautiful or successful poem, but it is the one in which he most fully reveals himself. An understanding of it is essential to an understanding of his most perfect poems, such as *The Garden*, *The Coronet* and the *Dialogue Between the Soul and the Body*. Characteristically, it contains many influences and echoes, including Christian platonism, the early Church fathers, and the poets Cleveland, Waller and Benlowes. Nevertheless, its real subject is Marvell's consideration of his position as the employee of Fairfax, the admired ex-general. The poem is therefore primarily a personal one: its profundities and its wisdom do not arise from a process of simply taking thought, but from the all-important process of living itself. And because Marvell was a poet, a poet of genius living in a period that was as difficult for poets as any has been, we can learn much from *Upon Appleton House* about the nature of poetry itself—about its relationship to experience and to action, about what it means (to poets) to be a poet, even about what poetry is.

Because Marvell is, like all poets, whether ostensibly or otherwise, talking about himself, his main theme here is retirement and action. He had written the *Horatian Ode* in 1650, probably before meeting Fairfax; there is an ironic bitterness about the opening of this poem, when he says that it is now time for the forward youth to forsake his dear muses, and leave the books in dust. By the time he came to write *Upon Appleton House* he was, we may reasonably infer, as contented as he ever was in his life—in retirement, and writing poetry, those who regard the opening lines of the *Ode* as totally without irony should note. Thus, *Upon Appleton House* lacks the bitter personal tone of a young man who is not at all sure what he is going to do. Marvell is in a happier position to make a sober consideration of the propriety of his own situation, and therefore of the relative virtues of poetic quietism and political activism. But although personal bitterness may be lacking, irony and nostalgic regret are not.

Upon Appleton House is at once a celebration of the gallant Fairfax's retirement to practise a wise quietism and an explanation of Marvell's own reluctant decision to pursue, in due course, a public rather than a private career. The poet's ecstatic description of his happiness in the woods and by the river of Nunappleton (LXI–LXXXI) is fraught with sadness and foreboding. Here, 'a great Prelate of the Grove', he is living in Paradise before the Fall; the unavoidable implication is that he has no more right to do this than any other man in difficult times. His reverie is interrupted (LXXXII) by the young Maria walking: she is his pupil, but she must grow up, and he must therefore eventually go. The outer world does not possess the 'decent Order tame' of this inner world, whose hopes are properly centred in Maria; nevertheless, Marvell, who unlike Fairfax had as yet achieved nothing in life, belongs to this outer world.

The sad but still playful final stanza depicts the poet entering the house of his host for the last time; it is a symbolic farewell to poetry, a decorous announcement of a resolution to translate poetic quietism into the kind of humble, virtuous action of which Fairfax is the prime exemplar.

At the conclusion of LXXXI, the point when his ecstatic reverie is interrupted by Maria, Marvell had described how the fishes 'twanged' at his lines; and how at the beginning of LXXXII he exclaims

> But now away my Hooks, my Quills,
> And Angles, idle Utensils.
> The *young Maria* walks to night . . .

By LXXXXVII, the final stanza, he sees himself, as a fisherman, hoisting his coracle over his head at dusk—and also he sees himself as reminded, at dusk, of such a sight (the 'dark *Hemisphere*' appearing like a coracle over the head), and consequently retreating into the blessed house.

A full exegesis of *Upon Appleton House* would demand many more pages than are in this book, for apart from its purely private allusions it contains literally thousands of references. It is one of the most learned poems in the language. But we believe that if it is carefully read along the lines we have suggested, with the help of the commentary we provide, its essential meaning will be grasped.

Thus a ready entrance is afforded into the unique richness of Marvell's finest poems. Structurally, as James Winny has pointed out in his useful selection, *Upon Appleton House* consists of seven sections: a description of the house (I–X), the history of 'the blooming Virgin Thwates', who eventually married Fairfax's ancestor (XI–XXXV), the description of the gardens (XXXVI–XLVI), of the adjoining meadows—the situation of the house (XLVII–LX), of the wood (LXI–LXXVIII), of the river (LXXIX–LXXXV), and of Mary Fairfax (LXXXVI–LXXXXVI).

Marvell is always a clever and intricate poet, whether he is writing the complex love lyrics for which he is most famous or railing satire (as in *The Character of Holland*, p. 113). He could no more help being clever than could his metaphysical predecessor, Donne. But he nearly always combines intellectual subtlety and wit with two other qualities: a sensuous celebration of natural beauty and an intense seriousness of feeling. He is not an easy poet; he is more difficult even than Donne, because, playful though he was, he lacks Donne's directness of approach, his attractive violence, his sheer animal enjoyment of his own brilliance and *joie de vivre*—in a word, his 'attack'.

But once Marvell's defences have been penetrated by the sensitive and careful reader, once it is understood that he uses poetry above all as an instrument to uncover the difficult truth, then he is revealed as, in Wordsworth's phrase, 'a man speaking to men'. He talks on a high level; he may have remained comparatively neglected for hundreds of years after his death because he marks the very end of a tradition rather than the beginning of a new one. Dryden, and Pope after him, regarded the usually insipid Waller as the main originator of the tradition in which they wrote; Dryden disliked Marvell, and Pope never mentioned him, although his poems had been published by T. Cooke in 1726. Yet no modern critic, however fashionably devoted to the Augustan tradition, would dream of preferring Waller to Marvell. Perhaps there is something to be learned from the fact that the Augustans themselves (with the honourable exception of Swift) could not appreciate Marvell. For it seems a poor tradition that can exist without him as an essential part.

This edition reprints all Marvell's English poems, and two extracts from his satirical verse. All but three of the poems appeared in the 1681 Folio (hereinafter referred to as F), whose order we follow. We also follow the text of F; all departures from it are indicated. We have collated our text with *The Poems of Andrew Marvell*, edited Hugh Macdonald, Routledge (1952), 1956 [Macdonald] and with the definitive edition, *Marvell's Poems and Letters*, edited H. M. Margoliouth, Clarendon Press, 2 volumes (1927), 1952 [M]. Apart from these, the chief collected editions of Marvell's poetry, to which we occasionally refer by the name of the editor, have been by T. Cooke (1726); E. Thompson (1776); A. B. Grosart (1872); G. A. Aitken (1892); Edward Wright (1904). Details of books and articles about Marvell, and selections, are given in the select bibliography (p. 11).

We should like to acknowledge the interest shown by Keith Nettle of Heinemann Educational Books, and to thank him for many helpful and constructive suggestions.

J. R.

M. S.-S.

SELECT BIBLIOGRAPHY

For editions of Marvell, see the note on the text at the end of the introduction.

SELECTIONS

Andrew Marvell: Selected Poetry and Prose, edited by Donald Davison, Harrap, 1952. This is a valuable selection, with a long and informative introduction. Unfortunately it is out of print. The notes to the poems are sparse.

Andrew Marvell: Some Poems, edited by James Winny, Hutchinson (1962), 1967. Some excellent notes.

BIOGRAPHY AND CRITICISM

P. Legouis, *André Marvell, Poète, Puritan, Patriote*, Paris, 1928. This was abridged and translated into English by the author as *Andrew Marvell, Poet, Puritan, Patriot*, Oxford University Press, 1965. The standard life.

M. C. Bradbrook and M. G. Lloyd Thomas, *Andrew Marvell*, Cambridge University Press, 1940. This is still the best critical and biographical study. (Referred to in commentary as MCB & MGL-T.)

J. B. Leishman, *The Art of Marvell's Poetry*, Hutchinson, 1966. Learned on Marvell's sources but continually misses the human point. (Referred to in commentary as L.)

John M. Wallace, *Destiny his Choice: The Loyalism of Andrew Marvell*, Cambridge University Press, 1967. The best book on Marvell's politics.

Christopher Hill, 'Society and Andrew Marvell' in *Puritanism and Revolution*, Secker & Warburg, 1958. An important essay by a distinguished historian.

Joan Bennett, 'Andrew Marvell' in *Five Metaphysical Poets*, Cambridge University Press (1934), 1964.

F. W. Bradbrook, 'The Poetry of Andrew Marvell' in *From Donne to Marvell*, edited B. Ford, Penguin, 1956.

Martin Seymour-Smith, 'Andrew Marvell' in *Poets Through their Letters*, Constable, 1969.

THE POEMS OF
ANDREW MARVELL

TO
THE READER

THESE are to Certifie every Ingenious Reader, that all these Poems, as also the other things in this Book contained, are Printed according to the exact Copies of my late dear Husband, under his own Hand-Writing, being found since his Death among his other Papers, Witness my Hand this 15th day of *October*, 1680.

Mary Marvell

A Dialogue between the Resolved Soul and Created Pleasure

COURAGE my Soul, now learn to wield
The weight of thine immortal Shield.
Close on thy Head thy Helmet bright.
Ballance thy Sword against the Fight.
See where an Army, strong as fair, 5
With silken Banners spreads the air.
Now, if thou bee'st that thing Divine,
In this day's Combat let it shine:
And shew that Nature wants an Art
To conquer one resolved Heart. 10

Pleasure

Welcome the Creations Guest,
Lord of Earth, and Heavens Heir.
Lay aside that Warlike Crest,
And of Nature's banquet share:
Where the Souls of fruits and flow'rs 15
Stand prepar'd to heighten yours.

Soul

I sup above, and cannot stay
To bait so long upon the way.

Pleasure

On these downy Pillows lye,
Whose soft Plumes will thither fly: 20
On these Roses strow'd so plain
Lest one Leaf thy Side should strain.

Soul

My gentler Rest is on a Thought,
Conscious of doing what I ought.

Pleasure

If thou bee'st with Perfumes pleas'd,   25
Such as oft the Gods appeas'd,
Thou in fragrant Clouds shalt show
Like another God below.

Soul

A Soul that knowes not to presume
Is Heaven's and its own perfume.   30

Pleasure

Every thing does seem to vie
Which should first attract thine Eye·
But since none deserves that grace,
In this Crystal view *thy* face.

Soul

When the Creator's skill is priz'd   35
The rest is all but Earth disguis'd.

Pleasure

Heark how Musick then prepares
For thy Stay these charming Aires;
Which the posting Winds recall,
And suspend the Rivers Fall.   40

Soul

Had I but any time to lose,
On this I would it all dispose.
Cease Tempter. None can chain a mind
Whom this sweet Chordage cannot bind.

Earth cannot shew so brave a Sight 45
As when a single Soul does fence
The Batteries of alluring Sense,
And Heaven views it with delight,
 Then persevere: for still new Charges sound:
 And if thou overcom'st thou shalt be crown'd. 50

Pleasure

All this fair, and soft, and sweet,
 Which scatteringly doth shine,
Shall within one Beauty meet,
 And she be only thine.

Soul

If things of Sight such Heavens be, 55
What Heavens are those we cannot see?

Pleasure

Where so e're thy Foot shall go
 The minted Gold shall lie;
Till thou purchase all below.
 And want new Worlds to buy. 60

Soul

Wer't not a price who'ld value Gold?
And that's worth nought that can be sold.

Pleasure

Wilt thou all the Glory have
 That War or Peace commend?
Half the World shall be thy Slave 65
 The other half thy Friend.

Soul

What Friends, if to my self untrue?
What Slaves, unless I captive you?

Pleasure

Thou shalt know each hidden Cause;
  And see the future Time: 70
Try what depth the Centre draws;
  And then to Heaven climb.

Soul

None thither mounts by the degree
Of Knowledge, but Humility.

Triumph, triumph, victorious Soul;   75
The World has not one Pleasure more:
The rest does lie beyond the Pole,
And is thine everlasting Store.

On a Drop of Dew

SEE how the Orient Dew,
Shed from the Bosom of the Morn
  Into the blowing Roses,
Yet careless of its Mansion new;
For the clear Region where 'twas born   5
  Round in its self incloses:
  And in its little Globes Extent,
Frames as it can its native Element.
How it the purple flow'r does slight,
  Scarce touching where it lyes,   10

But gazing back upon the Skies,
    Shines, with a mournful Light;
  Like its own Tear,
Because so long divided from the Sphear.
    Restless it roules and unsecure,   15
      Trembling lest it grow impure:
  Till the warm Sun pitty it's Pain,
And to the Skies exhale it back again.
      So the Soul, that Drop, that Ray
Of the clear Fountain of Eternal Day,   20
Could it within the humane flow'r be seen,
      Remembring still its former height,
      Shuns the sweat leaves and blossoms green
      And, recollecting its own Light,
Does, in its pure and circling thoughts, express   25
The greater Heaven in an Heaven less.
      In how coy a Figure wound,
      Every way it turns away:
      So the World excluding round,
      Yet receiving in the Day.   30
      Dark beneath, but bright above:
      Here disdaining, there in Love.
  How loose and easie hence to go:
  How girt and ready to ascend.
    Moving but on a point below,   35
    It all about does upwards bend.
Such did the Manna's sacred Dew destil;
White, and intire, though congeal'd and chill.
Congeal'd on Earth: but does, dissolving, run
Into the Glories of th' Almighty Sun.   40

The Coronet

WHEN for the Thorns with which I long, too long,
   With many a piercing wound,
   My Saviours head have crown'd,
I seek with Garlands to redress that Wrong:
   Through every Garden, every Mead,   5
I gather flow'rs (my fruits are only flow'rs)
   Dismantling all the fragrant Towers
That once adorned my Shepherdesses head.
And now when I have summ'd up all my store,
   Thinking (so I my self deceive)   10
   So rich a Chaplet thence to weave
As never yet the king of Glory wore:
   Alas I find the Serpent old
   That, twining in his speckled breast,
   About the flow'rs disguis'd does fold,   15
   With wreaths of Fame and Interest.
Ah, foolish Man, that would'st debase with them
And mortal Glory, Heaven's Diadem!
But thou who only could'st the Serpent tame,
Either his slipp'ry knots at once untie,   20
And disintangle all his winding Snare:
Or shatter too with him my curious frame:
And let these wither, so that he may die,
Though set with Skill and chosen out with Care.
That they, while Thou on both their Spoils dost tread,   25
May crown thy Feet, that could not crown thy Head.

Eyes and Tears

I

How wisely Nature did decree,
With the same Eyes to weep and see!
That, having view'd the object vain,
They might be ready to complain.

II

And, since the Self-deluding Sight,   5
In a false Angle takes each hight;
These Tears which better measure all,
Like wat'ry Lines and Plummets fall.

III

Two Tears, which Sorrow long did weigh
Within the Scales of either Eye,   10
And then paid out in equal Poise,
Are the true price of all my Joyes.

IV

What in the World most fair appears,
Yea even Laughter, turns to Tears:
And all the Jewels which we prize,   15
Melt in these Pendants of the Eyes.

V

I have through every Garden been,
Amongst the Red, the White, the Green;
And yet, from all the flow'rs I saw,
No Hony, but these Tears could draw.   20

VI

So the all-seeing Sun each day
Distills the World with Chymick Ray;
But finds the Essence only Showers,
Which straight in pity back he powers.

VII

Yet happy they whom Grief doth bless,   25
That weep the more, and see the less:
And, to preserve their Sight more true,
Bath still their Eyes in their own Dew.

VIII

*So *Magdalen*, in Tears more wise
Dissolv'd those captivating Eyes,   30
Whose liquid Chaines could flowing meet
To fetter her Redeemers feet.

IX

Not full sailes hasting loaden home,
Nor the chast Ladies pregnant Womb,
Nor *Cynthia* Teeming show's so fair,   35
As two Eyes swoln with weeping are.

X

The sparkling Glance that shoots Desire,
Drench'd in these Waves, does lose it fire.
Yea oft the Thund'rer pitty takes
And here the hissing Lightning slakes.   40

XI

The Incense was to Heaven dear,
Not as a Perfume, but a Tear.
And Stars shew lovely in the Night,
But as they seem the Tears of Light.

Ope then mine Eyes your double Sluice,   45
And practise so your noblest Use.
For others too can see, or sleep;
But only humane Eyes can weep.

XIII

Now like two Clouds dissolving, drop,
And at each Tear in distance stop: 50
Now like two Fountains trickle down:
Now like two floods o'return and drown.

XIIII

Thus let your Streams o'reflow your Springs,
Till Eyes and Tears be the same things:
And each the other's difference bears;   55
These weeping Eyes, those seeing Tears.

*Magdala, *lascivos sic quum dimisit Amantes,*
   Fervidaque in castas lumina solvit aquas;
Hæsit in irriguo lachrymarum compede Christus,
   Et tenuit sacros uda Catena pedes.   60

Bermudas

WHERE the remote *Bermudas* ride
In th' Oceans bosome unespy'd,
From a small Boat, that row'd along,
The listning Winds receiv'd this Song.
   What should we do but sing his Praise   5
That led us through the watry Maze,
Unto an Isle so long unknown,

And yet far kinder than our own?
Where he the huge Sea-Monsters wracks,
That lift the Deep upon their Backs.   10
He lands us on a grassy Stage;
Safe from the Storms, and Prelat's rage.
He gave us this eternal Spring,
Which here enamells every thing;
And sends the Fowl's to us in care,   15
On daily Visits through the Air.
He hangs in shades the Orange bright,
Like golden Lamps in a green Night.
And does in the Pomgranates close,
Jewels more rich than *Ormus* show's.   20
He makes the Figs our mouths to meet;
And throws the Melons at our feet.
But Apples plants of such a price,
No Tree could ever bear them twice.
With Cedars, chosen by his hand,   25
From *Lebanon*, he stores the Land.
And makes the hollow Seas, that roar,
Proclaime the Ambergris on shoar.
He cast (of which we rather boast)
The Gospels Pearl upon our Coast.   30
And in these Rocks for us did frame
A Temple, where to sound his Name.
Oh let our Voice his Praise exalt,
Till it arrive at Heavens Vault:
Which thence (perhaps) rebounding, may   35
Eccho beyond the *Mexique Bay*.
Thus sung they, in the *English* boat,
An holy and a chearful Note,
And all the way, to guide their Chime,
With falling Oars they kept the time.   40

Clorinda and Damon

C. *DAMON* come drive thy flocks this way.
D. No: 'tis too late they went astray.
C. I have a grassy Scutcheon spy'd,
   Where *Flora* blazons all her pride.
   The Grass I aim to feast thy Sheep: 5
   The Flow'rs I for thy Temples keep.
D. Grass withers; and the Flow'rs too fade.
C. Seize the short Joyes then, ere they vade.
   Seest thou that unfrequented Cave?
D. That den? C. Loves Shrine. D. But Virtue's Grave.   10
C. In whose cool bosome we may lye
   Safe from the Sun. D. not Heaven's Eye.
C. Near this, a Fountaines liquid Bell
   Tinkles within the concave Shell.
D. Might a Soul bath there and be clean,   15
   Or slake its Drought? C. What is't you mean?
D. These once had been enticing things,
   Clorinda, Pastures, Caves, and Springs.
C. And what late change? D. The other day
   Pan met me. C. What did great *Pan* say?   20
D. Words that transcend poor Shepherds skill.
   But He ere since my Songs does fill:
   And his Name swells my slender Oate.
C. Sweet must *Pan* sound in *Damons* Note.
D. *Clorinda's* voice might make it sweet.   25
C. Who would not in *Pan's* Praises meet?

CHORUS
Of Pan *the flowry Pastures sing,*
Caves eccho, and the Fountains ring.

Sing then while he doth us inspire;
For all the World is our Pan's *Quire.*

A Dialogue between the Soul and Body

Soul

O WHO shall, from this Dungeon, raise
A Soul inslav'd so many wayes?
With bolts of Bones, that fetter'd stands
In Feet; and manacled in Hands.
Here blinded with an Eye; and there   5
Deaf with the drumming of an Ear.
A Soul hung up, as 'twere, in Chains
Of Nerves, and Arteries, and Veins.
Tortur'd, besides each other part,
In a vain Head, and double Heart.   10

Body

O who shall me deliver whole,
From bonds of this Tyrannic Soul?
Which, stretcht upright, impales me so,
That mine own Precipice I go;
And warms and moves this needless Frame: 15
(A fever could but do the same.)
And, wanting where its spight to try,
Has made me live to let me dye.
A Body that could never rest,
Since this ill Spirit it possest.   20

Soul

What Magick could me thus confine
Within anothers Grief to pine?

Where whatsoever it complain,
I feel, that cannot feel, the pain.
And all my Care its self employes,   25
That to preserve, which me destroys:
Constrain'd not only to indure
Diseases, but, whats worse, the Cure:
And ready oft the Port to gain,
Am Shipwrackt into Health again.   30

Body
But Physick yet could never reach
The Maladies Thou me dost teach;
Whom first the Cramp of Hope does Tear:
And then the Palsie Shakes of Fear.
The Pestilence of Love does heat: 35
Or Hatred's hidden Ulcer eat.
Joy's chearful Madness does perplex:
Or Sorrow's other Madness vex.
Which Knowledge forces me to know;
And Memory will not foregoe.   40
What but a Soul could have the wit
To build me up for Sin so fit?
So Architects do square and hew,
Green Trees that in the Forest grew.

The Nymph complaining for the death of her Faun

THE wanton Troopers riding by
Have shot my Faun and it will dye.
Ungentle men! They cannot thrive
To kill thee. Thou neer didst alive

Them any harm: alas nor cou'd   5
Thy death yet do them any good.
I'me sure I never wisht them ill;
Nor do I for all this; nor will:
But, if my simple Pray'rs may yet
Prevail with Heaven to forget   10
Thy murder, I will Joyn my Tears
Rather then fail. But, O my fears!
It cannot dye so. Heavens King
Keeps register of every thing;
And nothing may we use in vain.   15
Ev'n Beasts must be with justice slain;
Else Men are made their *Deodands.*
Though they should wash their guilty hands
In this warm life blood, which doth part
From thine, and wound me to the Heart,   20
Yet could they not be clean: their Stain
Is dy'd in such a Purple Grain.
There is not such another in
The World, to offer for their Sin.

   Unconstant *Sylvio*, when yet   25
I had not found him counterfeit,
One morning (I remember well)
Ty'd in this silver Chain and Bell,
Gave it to me: nay and I know
What he said then; I'me sure I do.   30
Said He, look how your Huntsman here
Hath taught a Faun to hunt his *Dear.*
But *Sylvio* soon had me beguil'd.
This waxed tame; while he grew wild,
And quite regardless of my Smart,   35
Left me his Faun, but took his Heart.

   Thenceforth I set my self to play
My solitary time away,
With this: and very well content,

Could so mine idle Life have spent.   40
For it was full of sport; and light
Of foot, and heart; and did invite,
Me to its game: it seem'd to bless
Its self in me. How could I less
Than love it? O I cannot be   45
Unkind, t' a Beast that loveth me.

 Had it liv'd long, I do not know
Whether it too might have done so
As *Sylvio* did: his Gifts might be
Perhaps as false or more than he.   50
But I am sure, for ought that I
Could in so short a time espie,
Thy Love was far more better then
The love of false and cruel men.

 With sweetest milk, and sugar, first   55
I it at mine own fingers nurst.
And as it grew, so every day
It wax'd more white and sweet then they.
It had so sweet a Breath! And oft
I blusht to see its foot more soft,   60
And white, (shall I say then my hand?)
NAY any Ladies of the Land.

 It is a wond'rous thing, how fleet
'Twas on those little silver feet.
With what a pretty skipping grace,   65
It oft would challenge me the Race:
And when 'thad left me far away,
'Twould stay, and run again, and stay.
For it was nimbler much than Hindes;
And trod, as on the four Winds.   70

 I have a Garden of my own,
But so with Roses over grown,
And Lillies, that you would it guess
To be a little Wilderness.

And all the Spring time of the year   75
It onely loved to be there.
Among the beds of Lillyes, I
Have sought it oft, where it should lye;
Yet could not, till it self would rise,
Find it, although before mine Eyes.   80
For, in the flaxen Lillies shade,
It like a bank of Lillies laid.
Upon the Roses it would feed,
Until its Lips ev'n seem'd to bleed:
And then to me 'twould boldly trip,   85
And print those Roses on my Lip.
But all its chief delight was still
On Roses thus its self to fill:
And its pure virgin Limbs to fold
In whitest sheets of Lillies cold.   90
Had it liv'd long, it would have been
Lillies without, Roses within.

  O help! O help! I see it faint:
And dye as calmely as a Saint.
See how it weeps. The Tears do come   95
Sad, slowly dropping like a Gumme.
So weeps the wounded Balsome: so
The holy Frankincense doth flow.
The brotherless *Heliades*
Melt in such Amber Tears as these.   100

  I in a golden Vial will
Keep these two crystal Tears; and fill
It till it do o'reflow with mine;
Then place it in *Diana's* Shrine.

  Now my sweet Faun is vanish'd to   105
Whether the Swans and Turtles go:
In fair *Elizium* to endure,
With milk-white Lambs, and Ermins pure.
O do not run too fast: for I

Will but bespeak they Grave, and dye.   110
  First my unhappy Statue shall
Be cut in Marble; and withal,
Let it be weeping too: but there
Th' Engraver sure his Art may spare;
For I so truly thee bemoane,   115
That I shall weep though I be Stone:
Until my Tears, still dropping, wear
My breast, themselves engraving there.
There at my feet shalt thou be laid,
Of purest Alabaster made: 120
For I would have thine Image be
White as I can, though not as Thee.

Young Love

I

COME little Infant, Love me now,
  While thine unsuspected years
Clear thine aged Fathers brow
  From cold Jealousie and Fears.

II

Pretty surely 'twere to see   5
  By young Love old Time beguil'd:
While our Sportings are as free
  As the Nurses with the Child.

III

Common beauties stay fifteen;
  Such as yours should swifter move;   10
Whose fair Blossoms are too green
  Yet for Lust, but not for Love.

IV

Love as much the snowy Lamb
　　Or the wanton Kid does prize,
As the lusty Bull or Ram,　　　　　　　　　15
　　For his morning Sacrifice.

V

Now then love me: time may take
　　Thee before thy time away:
Of this Need wee'l Virtue make,
　　And learn Love before we may.　　　　　20

VI

So we win of doubtful Fate;
　　And, if good she to us meant,
We that Good shall antedate,
　　Or, if ill, that Ill prevent.

VII

Thus as Kingdomes, frustrating　　　　　　25
　　Other Titles to their Crown,
In the craddle crown their King,
　　So all Forraign Claims to drown,

VIII

So, to make all Rivals vain,
　　Now I crown thee with my Love:　　　　30
Crown me with thy Love again,
　　And we both shall Monarchs prove.

To his Coy Mistress

HAD we but World enough, and Time,
This coyness Lady were no crime.
We would sit down, and think which way
To walk, and pass our long Loves Day.
Thou by the *Indian Ganges* side   5
Should'st Rubies find: I by the Tide
Of *Humber* would complain. I would
Love you ten years before the Flood:
And you should if you please refuse
Till the Conversion of the *Jews*.   10
My vegetable Love should grow
Vaster then Empires, and more slow.
An hundred years should go to praise
Thine Eyes, and on thy Forehead Gaze.
Two hundred to adore each Breast: 15
But thirty thousand to the rest.
An Age at least to every part,
And the last Age should show your Heart.
For Lady you deserve this State;
Nor would I love at lower rate.   20
  But at my back I alwaies hear
Times winged Charriot hurrying near:
And yonder all before us lye
Desarts of vast Eternity.
Thy Beauty shall no more be found,   25
Nor, in thy marble Vault, shall sound
My ecchoing Song: then Worms shall try
That long preserv'd Virginity:

And your quaint Honour turn to dust;
And into ashes all my Lust.   30
The Grave's a fine and private place,
But none I think do there embrace.
   Now therefore, while the youthful hew
Sits on thy skin like morning glew,
And while thy willing Soul transpires   35
At every pore with instant Fires,
Now let us sport us while we may;
And now, like am'rous birds of prey,
Rather at once our Time devour,
Than languish in his slow-chapt pow'r.   40
Let us roll all our Strength, and all
Our sweetness, up into one Ball:
And tear our Pleasures with rough strife,
Thorough the Iron gates of Life.
Thus, though we cannot make our Sun   45
Stand still, yet we will make him run.

The Unfortunate Lover

I

ALAS, how pleasant are their dayes
With whom the Infant Love yet playes!
Sorted by pairs, they still are seen
By Fountains cool, and Shadows green.
But soon these Flames do lose their light,   5
Like Meteors of a Summers night:
Nor can they to that Region climb,
To make impression upon Time.

II

'Twas in a Shipwrack, when the Seas
Rul'd, and the Winds did what they please,　　　10
That my poor Lover floting lay,
And, e're brought forth, was cast away:
Till at the last the master-Wave
Upon the Rock his Mother drave;
And there she split against the Stone,　　　15
In a *Cesarian Section*.

III

The Sea him lent these bitter Tears,
Which at his Eyes he alwaies bears.
And from the Winds the Sighs he bore,
Which through his surging Breast do roar.　　　20
No Day he saw but that which breaks,
Through frighted Clouds in forked streaks.
While round the ratling Thunder hurl'd,
As at the Fun'ral of the World.

IV

While Nature to his Birth presents　　　25
This masque of quarrelling Elements;
A num'rous fleet of Corm'rants black,
That sail'd insulting o're the Wrack,
Receiv'd into their cruel Care,
Th' unfortunate and abject Heir:　　　30
Guardians most fit to entertain
The Orphan of the *Hurricane*.

V

They fed him up with Hopes and Air,
Which soon digested to Despair.
And as one Corm'rant fed him, still　　　35
Another on his Heart did bill.

Thus while they famish him, and feast,
He both consumed, and increast:
And languished with doubtful Breath,
Th' *Amphibium* of Life and Death.   40

VI

And now, when angry Heaven wou'd
Behold a spectacle of Blood,
Fortune and He are call'd to play
At sharp before it all the day:
And Tyrant Love his brest does ply   45
With all his wing'd Artillery.
Whilst he, betwixt the Flames and Waves,
Like *Ajax*, the mad Tempest braves.

VII

See how he nak'd and fierce dost stand,
Cuffing the Thunder with one hand;   50
While with the other he does lock,
And grapple, with the stubborn Rock:
From which he with each Wave rebounds,
Torn into Flames, and ragg'd with Wounds.
And all he saies, a Lover drest   55
In his own Blood does relish best.

VIII

This is the only *Banneret*
That ever Love created yet:
Who though, by the Malignant Starrs,
Forced to live in Storms and Warrs;   60
Yet dying leaves a Perfume here,
And Musick within every Ear:
And he in Story only rules,
In a Field *Sable* a Lover *Gules*.

36

The Gallery

I

CLORA come view my Soul, and tell
Whether I have contriv'd it well.
Now all its several lodgings lye
Compos'd into one Gallery;
And the great *Arras*-hangings, made 5
Of various Faces, by are laid;
That, for all furniture, you'l find
Only your Picture in my Mind.

II

Here Thou art painted in the Dress
Of an Inhumane Murtheress; 10
Examining upon our Hearts
Thy fertile Shop of cruel Arts:
Engines more keen than ever yet
Adorned Tyrants Cabinet;
Of which the most tormenting are 15
Black Eyes, red Lips, and curled Hair.

III

But, on the other side, th' art drawn
Like to *Aurora* in the Dawn;
When in the East she slumb'ring lyes,
And stretches out her milky Thighs; 20
While all the morning Quire does sing,
And *Manna* falls, and Roses spring;
And, at thy Feet, the wooing Doves
Sit perfecting their harmless Loves.

IV

Like an Enchantress here thou show'st,   25
Vexing thy restless Lover's Ghost;
And, by a Light obscure, dost rave
Over his Entrails, in the Cave;
Diving thence, with horrid Care,
How long thou shalt continue fair;   30
And (when inform'd) them throw'st away,
To be the greedy Vultur's prey.

V

But, against that, thou sit'st a float
Like *Venus* in her pearly Boat.
The *Halcyons*, calming all that's nigh,   35
Betwixt the Air and Water fly.
Or, if some rowling Wave appears,
A Mass of Ambergris it bears.
Nor blows more Wind than what may well
Convoy the Perfume to the Smell.   40

VI

These Pictures and a thousand more,
Of Thee, my Gallery dost store;
In all the Forms thou can'st invent
Either to please me, or torment:
For thou alone to people me,   45
Art grown a num'rous Colony;
And a Collection choicer far
Then or *White-hall's*, or *Mantua's* were.

VII

But, of these Pictures and the rest,
That at the Entrance likes me best: 50
Where the same Posture, and the Look
Remains, with which I first was took.

A tender Shepherdess, whose Hair
Hangs loosely playing in the Air,
Transplanting Flow'rs from the green Hill,   55
To crown her Head, and Bosome fill.

The Fair Singer

To make a final conquest of all me,
Love did compose so sweet an Enemy,
In whom both Beauties to my death agree,
Joyning themselves in fatal Harmony;
That while she with her Eyes my Heart does bind,   5
She with her Voice might captivate my Mind.

II
I could have fled from One but singly fair:
My dis-intangled Soul it self might save,
Breaking the curled trammels of her hair.
But how should I avoid to be her Slave,   10
Whose subtile Art invisibly can wreath
My Fetters of the very Air I breath?

III
It had been easy fighting in some plain,
Where Victory might hang in equal choice.
But all resistance against her is vain,   15
Who has th' advantage both of Eyes and Voice.
And all my Forces needs must be undone,
She having gained both the Wind and Sun.

Mourning

I

You, that decipher out the Fate
Of humane Off-springs from the Skies,
What mean these Infants which of late
Spring from the Starrs of *Chlora's* Eyes?

II

Her Eyes confus'd, and doubled ore,   5
With Tears suspended ere they flow;
Seem bending upwards, to restore
To Heaven, whence it came, their Woe.

III

When, molding of the watry Sphears,
Slow drops unty themselves away;   10
As if she, with those precious Tears,
Would strow the ground where *Strephon* lay.

IV

Yet some affirm, pretending Art,
Her Eyes have so her Bosome drown'd,
Only to soften near her Heart   15
A place to fix another Wound.

V

And, while vain Pomp does her restrain
Within her solitary Bowr,
She courts her self in am'rous Rain;
Her self both *Danae* and the Showr.   20

40

VI

Nay others, bolder, hence esteem
Joy now so much her Master grown,
That whatsoever does but seem
Like Grief, is from her Windows thrown.

VII

Nor that she payes, while she survives,   25
To her dead Love this Tribute due;
But casts abroad these Donatives,
At the installing of a new.

VIII

How wide they dream! The *Indian* Slaves
That sink for Pearl through Seas profound,   30
Would find her Tears yet deeper Waves
And not of one the bottom sound.

IX

I yet my silent Judgment keep,
Disputing not what they believe:
But sure as oft as Women weep,   35
It is to be suppos'd they grieve.

Daphnis and Chloe

I

DAPHNIS must from *Chloe* part:
Now is come the dismal Hour
That must all his Hopes devour,
All his Labour, all his Art.

II

Nature, her own Sexes foe,   5
Long had taught her to be coy:
But she neither knew t'enjoy,
Nor yet let her Lover go.

III

But, with this sad News surpriz'd,
Soon she let that Niceness fall;   10
And would gladly yield to all,
So it had his stay compriz'd.

IV

Nature so her self does use
To lay by her wonted State,
Lest the World should separate;   15
Sudden Parting closer glews.

V

He, well read in all the wayes
By which men their Siege maintain,
Knew not that the Fort to gain
Better 'twas the Siege to raise.   20

VI

But he came so full possest
With the Grief of Parting thence,
That he had not so much Sence
As to see he might be blest.

VII

Till Love in her Language breath'd   25
Words she never spake before;
But then Legacies no more
To a dying Man bequeath'd.

42

VIII

For, Alas, the time was spent,
Now the last minut's run
When poor *Daphnis* is undone,
Between Joy and Sorrow rent.

30

IX

At that *Why*, that *Stay my Dear*,
His disorder'd Locks he tare;
And with rouling Eyes did glare,
And his cruel fate forswear.

35

X

As the Soul of one scarce dead,
With the shrieks of Friends aghast,
Looks distracted back in hast,
And then streight again is fled.

40

XI

So did wretched *Daphnis* look,
Frighting her he loved most.
At the last, this Lovers Ghost
Thus his Leave resolved took.

XII

Are my Hell and Heaven Joyn'd
More to torture him that dies?
Could departure not suffice,
But that you must then grow kind?

45

XIII

Ah my *Chloe* how have I
Such a wretched minute found,
When they Favours should me wound
More than all thy Cruelty?

50

XIV

So to the condemned Wight
The delicious Cup we fill;
And allow him all he will,   55
For his last and short Delight.

XV

But I will not now begin
Such a Debt unto my Foe;
Nor to my Departure owe
What my Presence could not win.   60

XVI

Absence is too much alone:
Better 'tis to go in peace,
Than my Losses to increase
By a late Fruition.

XVII

Why should I enrich my Fate?   65
'Tis a Vanity to wear,
For my Executioner,
Jewels of so high a rate.

XVIII

Rather I away will pine
In a manly stubborness   70
Than be fatted up express
For the *Canibal* to dine.

XIX

Whilst this grief does thee disarm,
All th' Enjoyment of our Love
But the ravishment would prove   75
Of a Body dead while warm.

XX

And I parting should appear
Like the Gourmand *Hebrew* dead,
While with Quailes and *Manna* fed,
He does through the Desert err.   80

XXI

Or the Witch that midnight wakes
For the Fern, whose magick Weed
In one minute casts the Seed,
And invisible him makes.

XXII

Gentler times for Love are ment: 85
Who for parting pleasure strain
Gather Roses in the rain,
Wet themselves and spoil their Scent.

XXIII

Farewel therefore all the fruit
Which I could from Love receive: 90
Joy will not with Sorrow weave,
Nor will I this Grief pollute.

XXIV

Fate I come, as dark, as sad,
As thy Malice could desire;
Yet bring with me all the Fire   95
That Love in his Torches had.

XXV

At these words away he broke;
As who long has praying ly'n,
To his Heads-man makes the Sign,
And receives the parting stroke.   100

But hence Virgins all beware.
Last night he with *Phlogis* slept;
This night for *Dorinda* kept;
And but rid to take the Air.

Yet he does himself excuse;   105
Nor indeed without a Cause.
For, according to the Lawes,
Why did *Chloe* once refuse?

The Definition of Love

I

MY Love is of a birth as rare
As 'tis for object strange and high:
It was begotten by despair
Upon Impossibility.

II

Magnanimous Despair alone   5
Could show me so divine a thing,
Where feeble Hope could ne'r have flown
But vainly flapt its Tinsel Wing.

III

And yet I quickly might arrive
Where my extended Soul is fixt,   10
But Fate does Iron wedges drive,
And alwaies crouds it self betwixt.

For Fate with jealous Eye does see
Two perfect Loves; nor lets them close:
Their union would her ruine be,   15
And her Tyrannick pow'r depose.

And therefore her Decrees of Steel
Us as the distant Poles have plac'd,
(Though Loves whole World on us doth wheel)
Not by themselves to be embrac'd.   20

Unless the giddy Heaven fall,
And Earth some new Convulsion tear;
And, us to joyn, the World should all
Be cramp'd into a *Planisphere*.

As Lines so Loves *oblique* may well   25
Themselves in every Angle greet:
But ours so truly *Paralel*,
Though infinite can never meet.

Therefore the Love which us doth bind,
But Fate so enviously debarrs,   30
Is the Conjunction of the Mind,
And Opposition of the Stars.

The Picture of little T.C. in a Prospect of Love

I

SEE with what simplicity
This Nimph begins her golden daies!
In the green Grass she loves to lie,
And there with her fair Aspect tames
The Wilder flow'rs, and gives them names: 5
But only with the Roses playes;
        And them does tell
What Colour best becomes them, and what Smell.

II

Who can foretel for what high cause
This Darling of the Gods was born!   10
Yet this is She whose chaster Laws
The wanton Love shall one day fear,
And, under her command severe,
See his Bow broke and Ensigns torn.
        Happy, who can   15
Appease this virtuous Enemy of Man!

III

O then let me in time compound,
And parly with those conquering Eyes;
Ere they have try'd their force to wound,
Ere, with their glancing wheels, they drive   20
In Triumph over Hearts that strive,
And them that yield but more despise.
        Let me be laid,
Where I may see thy Glories from some Shade.

Mean time, whilst every verdant thing   25
It self does at thy Beauty charm,
Reform the errours of the Spring;
Make that the Tulips may have share
Of sweetness, seeing they are fair;
And Roses of their thorns disarm;   30
        But most procure
That Violets may a longer Age endure.

But O young beauty of the Woods,
Whom Nature courts with fruits and flow'rs,
Gather the Flow'rs, but spare the Buds;   35
Lest *Flora* angry at thy crime,
To kill her Infants in their prime,
Do quickly make th' Example Yours;
        And, ere we see,
Nip in the blossome all our hopes and Thee.   40

Tom May's Death

As one put drunk into the Packet-boat,
Tom May was hurry'd hence and did not know't.
But was amaz'd on the Elysian side,
And with an Eye uncertain, gazing wide,
Could not determine in what place he was,   5
For whence in Stevens ally Trees or Grass.
Nor where the Popes head, nor the Mitre lay,
Signs by which still he found and lost his way.
At last while doubtfully he all compares,
He saw near hand, as he imagin'd *Ares*.   10

Such did he seem for corpulence and port,
But 'twas a man much of another sort;
'Twas *Ben* that in the dusky Laurel shade
Amongst the Chorus of old Poets laid,
Sounding of ancient Heroes, such as were   15
The Subjects Safety, and the Rebel's Fear.
But how a double headed Vulture Eats,
Brutus and *Cassius* the Peoples cheats.
But seeing *May* he varied streight his Song,
Gently to signifie that he was wrong.   20
Cups more then civil of *Emathian* wine,
I sing (said he) and the *Pharsalian* Sign,
Where the Historian of the Common-wealth
In his own Bowels sheath'd the conquering health.
By this *May* to himself and them was come,   25
He found he was translated, and by whom.
Yet then with foot as stumbling as his tongue
Prest for his place among the Learned throng.
But *Ben*, who knew not neither foe nor friend,
Sworn Enemy to all that do pretend,   30
Rose more than ever he was seen severe,
Shook his gray locks, and his own Bayes did tear
At this intrusion. Then with Laurel wand,
The awful Sign of his supream command.
At whose dread Whisk *Virgil* himself does quake,   35
And *Horace* patiently its stroke does take,
As he crowds in he whipt him ore the pate
Like *Pembroke* at the Masque, and then did rate.
   Far from these blessed shades tread back agen
Most servil' wit, and Mercenary Pen.   40
Polydore, Lucan, Allan, Vandale, Goth,
Malignant Poet and Historian both.
Go seek the novice Statesmen, and obtrude
On them some Romane cast similitude,
Tell them of Liberty, the Stories fine,   45

Until you all grow Consuls in your wine.
Or thou *Dictator* of the glass bestow
On him the *Cato*, this the *Cicero*.
Transferring old *Rome* hither in your talk,
As *Bethlem's* House did to *Loretto* walk.   50
Foul Architect that hadst not Eye to see
How ill the measures of these States agree.
And who by *Romes* example *England* lay,
Those but to *Lucan* do continue *May*.
But the nor Ignorance nor seeming good   55
Misled, but malice fixt and understood.
Because some one than thee more worthy weares
The sacred Laurel, hence are all these teares?
Must therefore all the World be set on flame,
Because a Gazet writer mist his aim?   60
And for a Tankard-bearing Muse must we
As for the Basket *Guelphs* and *Gibellines* be?
When the Sword glitters ore the Judges head,
And fear has Coward Churchmen silenced,
Then is the Poets time, 'tis then he drawes,   65
And single fights forsaken Vertues cause.
He, when the wheel of Empire, whirleth back,
And though the World's disjoined Axel crack,
Sings still of ancient Rights and better Times,
Seeks wretched good, arraigns successful Crimes.   70
But thou base man first prostituted hast
Our spotless knowledge and the studies chast
Apostatizing from our Arts and us,
To turn the Chronicler to *Spartacus*.
Yet wast thou taken hence with equal fate,   75
Before thou couldst great *Charles* his death relate.
But what will deeper wound thy little mind,
Hast left surviving *Davenant* still behind
Who laughs to see in this thy death renew'd,
Right Romane poverty and gratitude.   80

Poor Poet thou, and grateful Senate they,
Who thy last Reckoning did so largely pay.
And with the publick gravity would come,
When thou hadst drunk thy last to lead thee home.
If that can be thy home where *Spencer* lyes   85
And reverend *Chaucer*, but their dust does rise
Against thee, and expels thee from their side,
As th' Eagles Plumes from other birds divide.
Nor here thy shade must dwell, Return, Return,
Where Sulphrey *Phlegeton* does ever burn.   90
The *Cerberus* with all his Jawes shall gnash,
Megæra thee with all her Serpents lash.
Thou rivited unto *Ixion's* wheel
Shalt break, and the perpetual Vulture feel.
'Tis just what Torments Poets ere did feign,   95
Thou first Historically shouldst sustain.
    Thus by irrevocable Sentence cast,
    May only Master of these Revels past.
    And streight he vanisht in a Cloud of pitch,
    Such as unto the Sabboth bears the Witch.   100

The Match

I

NATURE had long a Treasure made
    Of all her choisest store;
Fearing, when She should be decay'd
    To beg in vain for more.

II

Her *Orientist* Colours there,   5
    And Essences most pure,
With sweetest Perfumes hoarded were,
    All as she thought secure.

III

She seldom them unlock'd, or us'd,
　　But with the nicest care;
For, with one grain of them diffus'd,
　　She could the World repair.

IV

But likeness soon together drew
　　What she did separate lay;
Of which one perfect Beauty grew,
　　And that was *Celia*.

V

Love wisely had of long fore-seen
　　That he must once grow old;
And therefore stor'd a Magazine,
　　To save him from the cold.

VI

He kept the several Cells repleat
　　With Nitre thrice refin'd;
The Naphta's and the Sulphurs heat,
　　And all that burns the Mind.

VII

He fortifi'd the double Gate,
　　And rarely thither came;
For, with one Spark of these, he streight
　　All Nature could inflame.

VIII

Till, by vicinity so long,
　　A nearer Way they sought;
And, grown magnetically strong
　　Into each other wrought.

Thus all his fewel did unite
  To make one fire high:
None ever burn'd so hot, so bright: 35
  And *Celia* that am I.

So we alone the happy rest,
  Whilst all the World is poor,
And have within our Selves possest
  All Love's and Nature's store.   40

The Mower against Gardens

LUXURIOUS Man, to bring his Vice in use,
  Did after him the World seduce:
And from the fields the Flow'rs and Plants allure,
  Where Nature was most plain and pure.
He first enclos'd within the Gardens square   5
  A dead and standing pool of Air:
And a more luscious Earth for them did knead,
  Which stupifi'd them while it fed.
The Pink grew then as double as his Mind;
  The nutriment did change the kind.   10
With strange perfumes he did the Roses taint.
  And Flow'rs themselves were taught to paint.
The Tulip, white, did for complexion seek;
  And learn'd to interline its cheek:
Its Onion root they then so high did hold,   15
  That one was for a Meadow sold.
Another World was search'd, through Oceans new,
  To find the *Marvel of Peru*.

And yet these Rarities might be allow'd,
   To Man, that sov'raign thing and proud;   20
Had he not dealt between the Bark and Tree,
   Forbidden mixtures there to see.
No Plant now knew the Stock from which it came;
   He grafts upon the Wild the Tame;
That the uncertain and adult'rate fruit   25
   Might put the Palate in dispute.
His green *Seraglio* has its Eunuchs too;
   Lest any Tyrant him out-doe.
And in the Cherry he does Nature vex,
   To procreate without a Sex.   30
'Tis all enforc'd; the Fountain and the Grot;
   While the sweet Fields do lye forgot:
Where willing Nature does to all dispence
   A wild and fragrant Innocence:
And *Fauns* and *Faryes* do the Meadows till,   35
   More by their presence than their skill.
Their Statues polish'd by some ancient hand,
   May to adorn the Gardens stand:
But howso'ere the Figures do excel,
   The *Gods* themselves with us do dwell.   40

Damon the Mower

I

HEARK how the Mower *Damon* Sung,
With love of *Juliana* stung!
While ev'ry thing did seem to paint
The Scene more fit for his complaint.
Like her fair Eyes the day was fair;   5
But scorching like his am'rous Care.

Sharp like his Sythe his Sorrow was,
And wither'd like his Hopes the Grass.

II

Oh what unusual Heats are here,
Which thus our Sun-burn'd Meadows sear! 10
The Grass-hopper its pipe gives ore;
And hamstring'd Frogs can dance no more.
But in the brook the green Frog wades;
And Grass-hoppers seek out the shades.
Only the Snake, that kept within, 15
Now glitters in its second skin.

III

This heat the Sun could never raise,
Nor Dog-star so inflame's the dayes.
It from an higher Beauty grow'th,
Which burns the Fields and Mower both: 20
Which made the Dog, and makes the Sun
Hotter then his own *Phaeton*.
Not *July* causeth these Extremes,
But *Juliana's* scorching beams.

IV

Tell me where I may pass the Fires 25
Of the hot day, or hot desires.
To what cool Cave shall I descend,
Or to what gelid Fountain bend?
Alas! I look for Ease in vain,
When Remedies themselves complain. 30
No moisture but my Tears do rest,
Nor Cold but in her Icy Breast.

V

How long wilt Thou, fair Shepheardess,
Esteem me, and my Presents less?

To thee the harmless Snake I bring,   35
Disarmed of its teeth and sting.
To Thee *Chameleons* changing-hue,
And Oak leaves tipt with hony due.
Yet Thou ungrateful hast not sought
Nor what they are, nor who them brought.   40

VI

I am the Mower *Damon*, known
Through all the Meadows I have mown.
On me the Morn her dew distills
Before her darling Daffadils.
And, if at Noon my toil me heat,   45
The Sun himself licks off my Sweat.
While, going home, the Ev'ning sweet
In cowslip-water bathes my feet.

VII

What, though the piping Shepherd stock
The plains with an unnum'red Flock,   50
This Sithe of mine discovers wide
More ground then all his Sheep do hide.
With this the golden fleece I shear
Of all these Closes ev'ry Year.
And though in Wooll more poor then they,   55
Yet am I richer far in Hay.

VIII

Nor am I so deform'd to sight,
If in my Sithe I looked right;
In which I see my Picture done,
As in a crescent Moon the Sun.   60
The deathless Fairyes take me oft
To lead them in their Danses soft:
And, when I tune my self to sing,
About me they contract their Ring.

How happy might I still have mow'd,   65
Had not Love here his Thistles sow'd!
But now I all the day complain,
Joyning my Labour to my Pain;
And with my Sythe cut down the Grass,
Yet still my Grief is where it was: 70
But, when the Iron blunter grows,
Sighing I whet my Sythe and Woes.

X

While thus he threw his Elbow round,
Depopulating all the Ground,
And, with his whistling Sythe, does cut   75
Each stroke between the Earth and Root,
The edged Stele by careless chance
Did into his own Ankle glance;
And there among the Grass fell down,
By his own Sythe, the Mower mown.   80

XI

Alas! said He, these hurts are slight
To those that dye by Loves despight.
With Shepherds-purse, and Clowns-all-heal,
The Blood I stanch, and Wound I seal.
Only for him no Cure is found,   85
Whom *Julianus* Eyes do wound.
'Tis death alone that this must do:
For Death thou art a Mower too.

The Mower to the Glo-Worms

I

Ye living Lamps, by whose dear light
The Nightingale does sit so late,
And studying all the Summer-night,
Her matchless Songs does meditate;

II

Ye Country Comets, that portend   5
No War, nor Prince's funeral,
Shining unto no higher end
Then to presage the Grasses fall;

III

Ye Glo-worms, whose officious Flame
To wandring Mowers shows the way,   10
That in the Night have lost their aim,
And after foolish Fires do stray;

IV

Your courteous Lights in vain you wast,
Since *Juliana* here is come,
For She my Mind hath so displac'd   15
That I shall never find my home.

The Mower's Song

I

My Mind was once the true survey
Of all these Medows fresh and gay;
And in the greenness of the Grass
Did see its Hopes as in a Glass;
When *Juliana* came, and She   5
What I do to the Grass, does to my Thoughts and Me.

II

But these, while I with Sorrow pine,
Grew more luxuriant still and fine;
That none one Blade of Grass you spy'd,
But had a Flower on either side;   10
When *Juliana* came, and She
What I do to the Grass, does to my Thoughts and Me.

III

Unthankful Medows, could you so
A fellowship so true forego,
And in your gawdy May-games meet,   15
While I lay trodden under feet?
When *Juliana* came, and She
What I do to the Grass, does to my Thoughts and Me.

IV

But what you in Compassion ought,
Shall now by my Revenge be wrought: 20
And Flowr's, and Grass, and I and all,
Will in one common Ruine fall.

For *Juliana* comes, and She
What I do to the Grass, does to my Thoughts and Me.

V

And thus, ye Meadows, which have been   25
Companions of my thoughts more green,
Shall now the Heraldry become
With which I shall adorn my Tomb;
For *Juliana* comes, and She
What I do to the Grass, does to my Thoughts and Me.   30

Ametas and Thestylis making Hay-Ropes

I

Ametas

THINK'ST Thou that this Love can stand,
Whilst Thou still dost say me nay?
Love unpaid does soon disband:
Love binds Love as Hay binds Hay.

II

Thestylis

Think'st Thou that this Rope would twine   5
If we both should turn one way?
Where both parties so combine,
Neither Love will twist nor Hay.

III

Ametas

Thus you vain Excuses find,
Which your selve and us delay: 10

And Love tyes a Womans Mind
Looser then with Ropes of Hay.

IV

Thestylis

What you cannot constant hope
Must be taken as you may.

V

Ametas

Then let's both lay by our Rope,
And go kiss within the Hay.   15

Musicks Empire

I

FIRST was the World as one great Cymbal made,
Where Jarring Windes to infant Nature plaid.
All Musick was a solitary sound,
To hollow Rocks and murm'ring Fountains bound.

II

Jubal first made the wilder Notes agree;   5
And *Jubal* tuned Musicks *Jubilee*:
He call'd the *Ecchoes* from their sullen Cell,
And built the Organs City where they dwell.

III

Each sought a consort in that lovely place;
And Virgin Trebles wed the manly Base.   10
From whence the Progeny of numbers new
Into harmonious Colonies withdrew.

Some to the Lute, some to the Viol went,
And others chose the Cornet eloquent.
These practising the Wind, and those the Wire,   15
To sing Mens Triumphs, or in Heavens quire.

V

Then Musick, the Mosaique of the Air,
Did of all these a solemn noise prepare:
With which She gain'd the Empire of the Ear,
Including all between the Earth and Sphear.   20

VI

Victorious sounds! yet here your Homage do
Unto a gentler Conqueror then you;
Who though He flies the Musick of his praise,
Would with you Heavens Hallelujahs raise

The Garden

I

How vainly men themselves amaze
To win the Palm, the Oke, or Bayes;
And their uncessant Labours see
Crown'd from some single Herb or Tree,
Whose short and narrow verged Shade   5
Does prudently their Toyles upbraid;
While all Flow'rs and all Trees do close
To weave the Garlands of repose.

II

Fair quiet, have I found thee here,
And Innocence thy Sister dear!   10

Mistaken long, I sought you then
In busie Companies of Men.
Your sacred Plants, if here below,
Only among the Plants will grow.
Society is all but rude,   15
To this delicious Solitude.

III

No white nor red was ever seen
So am'rous as this lovely green.
Fond Lovers, cruel as their Flame,
Cut in these Trees their Mistress name.   20
Little, Alas, they know, or heed,
How far these Beauties Hers exceed!
Fair Trees! where s'eer your barkes I wound,
No Name shall but your own be found.

IV

When we have run our Passions heat,   25
Love hither makes his best retreat.
The *Gods*, that mortal Beauty chase,
Still in a Tree did end their race.
Apollo hunted *Daphne* so,
Only that She might Laurel grow.   30
And *Pan* did after *Syrinx* speed,
Not as a Nymph, but for a Reed.

V

What wond'rous Life in this I lead!
Ripe Apples drop about my head;
The Luscious Clusters of the Vine   35
Upon my Mouth do crush their Wine;
The Nectaren, and curious Peach,
Into my hands themselves do reach;
Stumbling on Melons, as I pass,
Insnar'd with Flow'rs, I fall on Grass.   40

Mean while the Mind, from pleasure less,
Withdraws into its happiness:
The Mind, that Ocean where each kind
Does streight its own resemblance find;
Yet it creates, transcending these,   45
Far other Worlds, and other Seas;
Annihilating all that's made
To a green Thought in a green Shade.

VII

Here at the Fountains sliding foot,
Or at some Fruit-trees mossy root,   50
Casting the Bodies Vest aside,
My Soul into the boughs does glide:
There like a Bird it sits, and sings,
Then whets, and combs its silver Wings;
And, till prepar'd for longer flight,   55
Waves in its Plumes the various Light.

VIII

Such was that happy Garden-state,
While Man there walk'd without a Mate:
After a Place so pure, and sweet,
What other Help could yet be meet!   60
But 'twas beyond a Mortal's share
To wander solitary there:
Two Paradises t'were in one
To live in Paradise alone.

IX

How well the skilful Gardner drew   65
Of flow'rs and herbes this Dial new;
Where from above the milder Sun
Does through a fragrant Zodiack run;

And, as it works, th' industrious Bee
Computes its time as well as we.
How could such sweet and wholsome Hours
Be reckon'd but with herbs and flow'rs!

Fleckno, an English Priest at Rome

OBLIG'D by frequent visits of this man,
Whom as Priest, Poet, and Musician,
I for some branch of *Melchizedeck* took,
(Though he derives himself from *my Lord Brooke*)
I sought his Lodging; which is at the Sign
Of the sad *Pelican*; Subject divine
For Poetry: There three Stair-Cases high,
Which signifies his triple property,
I found at last a Chamber, as 'twas said,
But seem'd a Coffin set on the Stairs head.
Not higher than Seav'n, nor larger then three feet;
Only there was nor Seeling, nor a Sheet,
Save that th' ingenious Door did as you come
Turn in, and shew to Wainscot half the Room.
Yet of his State no man could have complain'd;
There being no Bed where he entertain'd:
And though within one Cell so narrow pent,
He'd *Stanza's* for a whole Appartement.

Straight without further information,
In hideous verse, he, and a dismal tone,
Begins to exorcise; as if I were
Possest; and sure the *Devil* brought me there.
But I, who now imagin'd my self brought
To my last Tryal, in a serious thought
Calm'd the disorders of my youthful Breast,

And to my Martyrdom prepared Rest.
Only this frail Ambition did remain,
The last distemper of the sober Brain,
That there had been some present to assure
The future Ages how I did indure;   30
And how I, silent, turn'd my burning Ear
Towards the Verse; and when that could not hear,
Held him the other; and unchanged yet,
Ask'd still for more, and pray'd him to repeat:
Till the Tyrant, weary to persecute,   35
Left off, and try'd t' allure me with his Lute.

 Now as two Instruments, to the same key
Being tun'd by Art, if the one touched be
The other opposite as soon replies,
Mov'd by the Air and hidden Sympathies;   40
So while he with his gouty Fingers craules
Over the Lute, his murmuring Belly calls,
Whose hungry Guts to the same streightness twin'd
In Echo to the trembling Strings repin'd.

 I, that perceiv'd now what his Musick ment, 45
Ask'd civilly if he had eat this Lent.
He answered yes; with such, and such an one.
For he has this of gen'rous, that alone
He never feeds; save only when he tryes
With gristly Tongue to dart the passing Flyes. 50
I ask'd if he eat flesh. And he, that was
So hungry that though ready to say *Mass*
Would break his fast before, said he was Sick,
And th' *Ordinance* was only Politick.
Nor was I longer to invite him: Scant   55
Happy at once to make him Protestant,
And Silent. Nothing now the Dinner stay'd
But till he had himself a Body made.
I mean till he were drest: for else so thin
He stands, as if he only fed had been   60

With consecrated Wafers; and the *Host*
Hath sure more flesh and blood then he can boast.
This *Basso Relievo* of a Man,
Who as a Camel tall, yet easly can
The Needles Eye thread without any stich,   65
(His only impossible is to be rich)
Lest his too suttle Body, growing rare,
Should leave his Soul to wander in the Air,
He therefore circumscribes himself in rimes;
And swaddled in's own papers seaven times,   70
Wears a close Jacket of poetick Buff,
With which he doth his third Dimension Stuff
Thus armed underneath, he over all
Does make a primitive *Sotana* fall;
And above that yet casts an antick Cloak,   75
Worn at the first Counsel of *Antioch*;
Which by the *Jews* long hid, and Disesteem'd,
He heard of by Tradition, and redeem'd.
But were he not in this black habit deck't,
This half transparent Man would soon reflect   80
Each colour that he past by; and be seen.
As the *Chamelion*, yellow, blew, or green.
　　He drest, and ready to disfurnish now
His Chamber, whose compactness did allow
No empty place for complementing doubt,   85
But who came last is forc'd first to go out;
I meet one on the Stairs who made me stand,
Stopping the passage, and did him demand:
I answer'd he is here *Sir*; but you see
You cannot pass to him but thorow me.   90
He thought himself affronted; and reply'd,
I whom the Pallace never has deny'd
Will make the way here; I said *Sir* you'l do
Me a great favour, for I seek to go.
He gathring fury still made sign to draw;   95

But himself there clos'd in a Scabbard saw
As narrow as his Sword's; and I, that was
Delightful, said there can no Body pass
Except by penetration hither, where
Two make a crowd, nor can three Persons here   100
Consist but in one substance. Then, to fit
Our peace, the Priest said I too had some wit:
To prov't, I said, the place doth us invite
By its own narrowness, Sir, to unite.
He ask'd me pardon; and to make my way   105
Went down, as I him follow'd to obey.
But the propitiatory Priest had straight
Oblig'd us, when below, to celebrate
Together our attonement: so increas'd
Betwixt us two the Dinner to a Feast.   110
Let it suffice that we could eat in peace;
And that both Poems did and Quarrels cease
During the Table; though my new made Friend
Did, as he threatened, ere 'twere long intend
To be both witty and valiant: I loth,   115
Said 'twas too late, he was already both.
    But now, Alas, my first Tormentor came,
Who satisfy'd with eating, but not tame
Turns to recite; though Judges most severe
After th' Assizes dinner mild appear,   120
And on full stomach do condemn but few:
Yet he more strict my sentence doth renew;
And draws out of the black box of his Breast
Ten quire of paper in which he was drest.
Yet that which was a greater cruelty   125
Then *Nero's* Poem he calls charity:
And so the *Pelican* at his door hung
Picks out the tender bosome to its young.
    Of all his Poems there he stands ungirt
Save only two foul copies for his shirt: 130
69

Yet these he promises as soon as clean.
But how I loath'd to see my Neighbour glean
Those papers, which he pilled from within
Like white fleaks rising from a Leaper's skin!
More odious then those raggs which the *French* youth   135
At ordinaries after dinner show'th,
When they compare their *Chancres* and *Poulains*.
Yet he first kist them, and after takes pains
To read; and then, because he understood
Not one Word, thought and swore that they were good.   140
But all his praises could not now appease
The provok't Author, whom it did displease
To hear his Verses, by so just a curse,
That were ill made condemn'd to be read worse:
And how (impossible) he made yet more   145
Absurdityes in them then were before.
For he his untun'd voice did fall or raise
As a deaf Man upon a Viol playes,
Making the half points and the periods run
Confus'der then the atomes in the Sun.   150
Thereat the Poet swell'd, with anger full,
And roar'd out, like *Perillus* in's own *Bull*;
Sir you read false. That any one but you
Should know the contrary. Whereat, I, now
Made Mediator, in my room, said, Why?   155
To say that you read false *Sir* is no Lye.
Thereat the waven Youth relented straight;
But saw with sad dispair that 'twas too late.
For the disdainful Poet was retir'd
Home, his most furious Satyr to have fir'd   160
Against the Rebel; who, at this struck dead,
Wept bitterly as disinherited.
Who should commend his Mistress now? Or who
Praise him? both difficult indeed to do
With truth. I counsell'd him to go in time,   165

Ere the fierce Poets anger turn'd to rime.
    He hasted; and I, finding my self free,
As one scap't strangely from Captivity,
Have made the Chance be painted; and go now
To hang it in *Saint Peter's* for a Vow.   170

To his worthy Friend Doctor Witty upon his Translation of the Popular Errors

Sit further, and make room for thine own fame,
Where just desert enrolles thy honour'd Name
The good Interpreter. Some in this task
Take of the Cypress vail, but leave a mask,
Changing the Latine, but do more obscure   5
That sence in *English* which was bright and pure.
So of Translators they are Authors grown,
For ill Translators make the Book their own.
Others do strive with words and forced phrase
To add such lustre, and so many rayes,   10
That but to make the Vessel shining, they
Much of the precious Metal rub away.
He is Translations thief that addeth more,
As much as he that taketh from the Store
Of the first Author. Here he maketh blots   15
That mends; and added beauties are but spots.
    Cælia whose English doth more richly flow
Then *Tagus*, purer then dissolved snow,
And sweet as are her lips that speak it, she
Now learns the tongues of *France* and *Italy*;   20
But she is *Cælia* still: no other grace

71

But her own smiles commend that lovely face;
Her native beauty's not Italianated,
Nor her chast mind into the *French* translated:
Her thoughts are *English*, though her sparkling wit   25
With other Language doth them fitly fit.
    Translators learn of her: but stay I slide
Down into Error with the Vulgar tide;
Women must not teach here: the Doctor doth
Stint them to Cawdles, Almond-milk, and Broth.   30
Now I reform, and surely so will all
Whose happy Eyes on thy Translation fall,
I see the people hastning to thy Book,
Liking themselves the worse the more they look,
And so disliking, that they nothing see   35
Now worth the liking, but thy Book and thee.
And (if I Judgment have) I censure right;
For something guides my hand that I must write.
You have Translations statutes best fulfil'd.
That handling neither sully nor would guild.   40

On Mr. Milton's Paradise Lost

WHEN I beheld the Poet blind, yet bold,
In slender Book his vast Design unfold,
Messiah Crown'd, *Gods* Reconcil'd Decree,
Rebelling *Angels*, the Forbidden Tree,
Heav'n, Hell, Earth, Chaos, All; the Argument   5
Held me a while misdoubting his Intent,
That he would ruine (for I saw him strong)
The sacred Truths to Fable and old Song,
(So *Sampson* groap'd the Temples Posts in spight)
The World o'rewhelming to revenge his Sight.   10

Yet as I read, soon growing less severe,
I lik'd his Project, the success did fear;
Through that wide Field how he his way should find
O're which lame Faith leads Understanding blind;
Lest he perplext the things he would explain,   15
And what was easie he should render vain.

Or if a Work so infinite he spann'd,
Jealous I was that some less skilful hand
(Such as disquiet alwayes what is well,
And by ill imitating would excell)   20
Might hence presume the whole Creations day
To change in Scenes, and show it in a Play.

Pardon me, *mighty Poet*, nor despise
My causeless, yet not impious, surmise.
But I am now convinc'd, and none will dare   25
Within thy Labours to pretend a Share.
Thou hast not miss'd one thought that could be fit,
And all that was improper dost omit:
So that no room is here for Writers left,
But to detect their Ignorance or Theft.   30

That Majesty which through thy Work doth Reign
Draws the Devout, deterring the Profane.
And things divine thou treatst of in such state
As them preserves, and Thee inviolate.
At once delight and horrour on us seize,   35
Thou singst with so much gravity and ease;
And above humane flight dost soar aloft,
With Plume so strong, so equal, and so soft.
The *Bird* nam'd from that *Paradise* you sing
So never Flags, but alwaies keeps on Wing.   40

Where couldst thou Words of such a compass find?
Whence furnish such a vast expense of Mind?
Just Heav'n Thee, like *Tiresias*, to requite,
Rewards with *Prophesie* thy loss of Sight.

Well mightst thou scorn thy Readers to allure   45

With tinkling Rhime, of thy own Sense secure;
While the *Town-Bays* writes all the while and spells,
And like a Pack-Horse tires without his Bells.
Their Fancies like our bushy Points appear,
The Poets rag them; we for fashion wear.   5C
I too transported by the *Mode* offend,
And while I meant to *Praise* thee, must Commend.
Thy verse created like thy *Theme* sublime,
In Number, Weight, and Measure, needs not *Rhime*.

Senec. Traged. ex Thyeste Chor. 2

Stet quicunque volet potens
Aulæ culmine lubrico *&c.*

Translated

CLIMB at *Court* for me that will
Tottering favors Pinacle;
All I see is to lye still.
Settled in some secret Nest
In calm Leisure let me rest;   S
And far off the publick Stage
Pass away my silent Age.
Thus when without noise, unknown,
I have liv'd out all my span,
I shall dye, without a groan,   IC
An old honest Country man.
Who expos'd to others Ey's,
Into his own Heart ne'r pry's,
Death to him's a Strange surprise.

74

An Epitaph upon ——

ENOUGH: and leave the rest to Fame.
'Tis to commend her but to name.
Courtship, which living she declin'd,
When dead to offer were unkind.
Where never any could speak ill,　　　　　5
Who would officious Praises spill?
Nor can the truest Wit or Friend,
Without Detracting, her commend.
To say she liv'd a *Virgin* chast,
In this Age loose and all unlac't;　　　　10
Nor was, when Vice is so allow'd,
Of *Virtue* or asham'd, or proud;
That her Soul was on *Heaven* so bent
No Minute but it came and went;
That ready her last Debt to pay　　　　　15
She summ'd her Life up ev'ry day;
Modest as Morn; as Mid-day bright;
Gentle as Ev'ning; cool as Night;
'Tis true; but all so weakly said;
'Twere more Significant, *She's Dead.*　　　20

Upon the Hill and Grove at Bill-borow

To the Lord Fairfax

I

SEE how the arched Earth does here
Rise in a perfect Hemisphere!

The stiffest Compass could not strike
A Line more circular and like;
Nor softest Pensel draw a Brow   5
So equal as this Hill does bow.
It seems as for a Model laid,
And that the World by it was made.

II

Here learn ye Mountains more unjust,
Which to abrupter greatness thrust,   10
That do with your hook-shoulder'd height
The Earth deform and Heaven fright.
For whose excrescence ill design'd,
Nature must a new Center find,
Learn here those humble steps to tread,   15
Which to securer Glory lead.

III

See what a soft access and wide
Lyes open to its grassy side;
Nor with the rugged path deterrs
The feet of breathless Travellers.   20
See then how courteous it ascends,
And all the way it rises bends;
Nor for it self the height does gain,
But only strives to raise the Plain.

IV

Yet thus it all the field commands,   25
And in unenvy'd Greatness stands,
Discerning farther then the Cliff
Of Heaven-daring *Teneriff.*
How glad the weary Seamen hast
When they salute it from the Mast!   30
By Night the Northern Star their way
Directs, and this no less by Day.

V

Upon its crest this Mountain grave
A Plump of aged Trees does wave.
No hostile hand durst ere invade
With impious Steel the sacred Shade.
For something alwaies did appear
Of the *great Masters* terrour there:
And Men could hear his Armour still
Ratling through all the Grove and Hill.

35

40

VI

Fear of the *Master*, and respect
Of the great *Nymph* did it protect;
Vera the *Nymph* that him inspir'd,
To whom he often here retir'd,
And on these Okes ingrav'd her Name;
Such Wounds alone these Woods became:
But ere he well the Barks could part
'Twas writ already in their Heart.

45

VII

For they ('tis credible) have sense,
As We, of Love and Reverence,
And underneath the Courser Rind
The *Genius* of the house do bind.
Hence they successes seem to know,
And in their *Lord's* advancement grow;
But in no Memory were seen
As under this so streight and green.

50

55

VIII

Yet now no further strive to shoot,
Contented if they fix their Root.
Nor to the winds uncertain gust,
Their prudent Heads too far intrust.

60

Onely sometimes a flutt'ring Breez
Discourses with the breathing Trees;
Which in their modest Whispers name
Those Acts that swell'd the Cheek of Fame.

IX

Much other Groves, say they, then these   65
And other Hills him once did please.
Through Groves of Pikes he thunder'd then,
And Mountains' rais'd of dying Men.
For all the *Civick Garlands* due
To him our Branches are but few.   70
Nor are our Trunks enow to bear
The *Trophees* of one fertile Year.

X

'Tis true, ye Trees nor ever spoke
More certain *Oracles* in Oak.
But Peace (if you his favour prize)   75
That Courage its own Praises flies.
Therefore to your obscurer Seats
From his own Brightness he retreats:
Nor he the Hills without the Groves,
Nor Height but with Retirement loves.   80

Upon Appleton House, to my Lord Fairfax

I

WITHIN this sober Frame expect
Work of no Forrain *Architect*;
That unto Caves the Quarries drew,
And Forrests did to Pastures hew;

Who of his great Design in pain   5
Did for a Model vault his Brain,
Whose Columnes should so high be rais'd
To arch the Brows that on them gaz'd.

II

Why should of all things Man unrul'd
Such unproportion'd dwellings build?   10
The Beasts are by their Denns exprest:
And Birds contrive an equal Nest;
The low roof'd Tortoises do dwell
In cases fit of Tortoise-shell:
No Creature loves an empty space;   15
Their Bodies measure out their Place.

III

But He, superfluously spread,
Demands more room alive then dead.
And in his hollow Palace goes
Where Winds as he themselves may lose.   20
What need of all this Marble Crust
T'impark the wanton Mole of Dust,
That thinks by Breadth the World t'unite
Though the first Builders fail'd in Height?

IV

But all things are composed here   25
Like Nature, orderly and near:
In which we the Dimensions find
Of that more sober Age and Mind,
When larger sized Men did stoop
To enter at a narrow loop;   30
As practising, in doors so strait,
To strain themselves through *Heavens Gate*.

V

And surely when the after Age
Shall hither come in *Pilgrimage*,
These sacred Places to adore,   35
By *Vere* and *Fairfax* trod before,
Men will dispute how their Extent
Within such dwarfish Confines went:
And some will smile at this, as well
As *Romulus* his Bee-like Cell.   40

VI

Humility alone designs
Those short but admirable Lines,
By which, ungirt and unconstrain'd,
Things greater are in less contain'd.
Let others vainly strive t'immure   45
The *Circle* in the *Quadrature*!
These *holy Mathematicks* can
In ev'ry Figure equal Man.

VII

Yet thus the laden House does sweat,
And scarce indures the *Master* great: 50
But where he comes the swelling Hall
Stirs, and the *Square* grows *Spherical*;
More by his *Magnitude* distrest,
Then he is by its straitness prest:
And too officiously it slights   55
That in it self which him delights.

VIII

So Honour better Lowness bears,
Then That unwonted Greatness wears.
Height with a certain Grace does bend,
But low Things clownishly ascend.   60

And yet what needs there here Excuse,
Where ev'ry Thing does answer Use?
Where neatness nothing can condemn,
Nor Pride invent what to contemn?

IX

A Stately *Frontispiece of Poor*   65
Adorns without the open Door:
Nor less the Rooms within commends
Daily new *Furniture of Friends*.
The House was built upon the Place
Only as for *a Mark of Grace*;   70
And for an *Inn* to entertain
Its *Lord* a while, but not remain.

X

Him *Bishops-Hill*, or *Denton* may,
Or *Bilbrough*, better hold then they:
But Nature here hath been so free   75
As if she said leave this to me.
Art would more neatly have defac'd
What she had laid so sweetly wast;
In fragrant Gardens, shaddy Woods,
Deep Meadows, and transparent Floods.   80

XI

While with slow Eyes we these survey,
And on each pleasant footstep stay,
We opportunly may relate
The Progress of this Houses Fate.
A *Nunnery* first gave it birth.   85
For *Virgin Buildings* oft brought forth.
And all that Neighbour-Ruine shows
The Quarries whence this dwelling rose.

XII

Near to this gloomy Cloysters Gates
There dwelt the blooming Virgin *Thwates*;   90
Fair beyond Measure, and an Heir
Which might Deformity make fair.
And oft She spent the Summer Suns
Discoursing with the *Suttle Nunns*.
Whence in these Words one to her weav'd,   95
(As 'twere by Chance) Thoughts long conceiv'd.

XIII

'Within this holy leisure we
'Live innocently as you see.
'These Walls restrain the World without,
'But hedge our Liberty about.   100
'These Bars inclose that wider Den
'Of those wild Creatures, called Men.
'The Cloyster outward shuts its Gates,
'And, from us, locks on them the Grates.

XIV

'Here we, in shining Armour white,   105
'Like *Virgin Amazons* do fight.
'And our chast *Lamps* we hourly trim,
'Lest the great *Bridegroom* find them dim.
'Our *Orient* Breaths perfumed are
'With insense of incessant Pray'r.   110
'And Holy-water of our Tears
'Most strangly our Complexion clears.

XV

'Not Tears of Grief; but such as those
'With which calm Pleasure overflows;
'Or Pity, when we look on you   115
'That live without this happy Vow.

'How should we grieve that must be seen
'Each one a *Spouse*, and each a *Queen*;
'And can in *Heaven* hence behold
'Our brighter Robes and Crowns of Gold?   120

XVI

'When we have prayed all our Beads,
'Some One the holy *Legend* reads;
'While all the rest with Needles paint
'The Face and Graces of the *Saint*.
'But what the Linnen can't receive   125
'They in their Lives do interweave.
'This Work the *Saints* best represents;
'That serves for *Altar's Ornaments*.

XVII

'But much it to our work would add
'If here your hand, your Face we had: 130
'By it we would *our Lady* touch;
'Yet thus She you rsembles much.
'Some of your Features, as we sow'd,
'Through ev'ry *Shrine* should be bestow'd.
'And in one Beauty we would take   135
'Enough a thousand *Saints* to make.

XVIII

'And (for I dare not quench the Fire
'That me does for your good inspire)
''Twere Sacriledge a Man t'admit
'To holy things, for *Heaven* fit.   140
'I see the *Angels* in a Crown
'On you the Lillies show'ring down:
'And round about you Glory breaks.
'That something more then humane speaks.

XIX

'All Beauty, when at such a height,   145
'Is so already consecrate.
'*Fairfax* I know; and long ere this
'Have mark'd the Youth, and what he is.
'But can he such a *Rival* seem
'For whom you *Heav'n* should disesteem?   150
'Ah, no! and 'twould more Honour prove
'He your *Devoto* were, then *Love*.

XX

'Here live beloved, and obey'd:
'Each one your Sister, each your Maid.
'And, if our Rule seem strictly pend,   155
'The Rule it self to you shall bend.
'Our *Abbess* too, now far in Age,
'Doth your succession near presage.
'How soft the yoke on us would lye,
'Might such fair Hands as yours it tye!   160

XXI

'Your voice, the sweetest of the Quire,
'Shall draw *Heav'n* nearer, raise us higher.
'And your Example, if our Head,
'Will soon us to perfection lead.
'Those Virtues to us all so dear,   165
'Will straight grow Sanctity when here:
'And that, once sprung, increase so fast
'Till Miracles it work at last.

XXII

'Nor is our *Order* yet so nice,
'Delight to banish as a Vice.   170
'Here Pleasure Piety doth meet;
'One perfecting the other Sweet.

'So through the mortal fruit we boyl
'The Sugars uncorrupting Oyl:
'And that which perisht while we pull,   175
'Is thus preserved clear and full.

XXIII

'For such indeed are all our Arts;
'Still handling Natures finest Parts.
'Flow'rs dress the Altars; for the Clothes,
'The Sea-born Amber we compose;   180
'Balms for the griv'd we draw; and Pasts
'We mold, as Baits for curious tasts.
'What need is here of Man? unless
'These as sweet Sins we should confess.

XXIV

'Each Night among us to your side   185
'Appoint a fresh and Virgin Bride;
'Whom if *our Lord* at midnight find,
'Yet Neither should be left behind.
'Where you may lye as chast in Bed
'As Pearls together billeted.   190
'All Night embracing Arm in Arm,
'Like Chrystal pure with Cottom warm.

XXV

'But what is this to all the store
'Of Joys you see, and may make more!
'Try but a while, if you be wise: 195
'The Tryal neither Costs, nor Tyes.
Now *Fairfax* seek her promis'd faith:
Religion that dispensed hath;
Which She hence forward does begin;
The *Nuns* smooth Tongue has suckt her in.   200

Oft, though he knew it was in vain,
Yet would he valiantly complain.
'Is this that *Sanctity* so great,
'An Art by which you finly'r cheat?
'Hypocrite Witches, hence *avant*,   205
'Who though in prison yet inchant!
'Death only can such Theeves make fast,
'As rob though in the Dungeon cast.

'Were there but, when this House was made,
'One Stone that a just Hand had laid,   210
'It must have fall'n upon her Head
'Who first Thee from thy Faith misled.
'And yet, how well soever ment,
'With them 'twould soon grow fraudulent:
'For like themselves they alter all,   215
'And vice infects the very Wall.

XXVIII

'But sure those Buildings last not long,
'Founded by Folly, kept by Wrong.
'I know what Fruit their Gardens yield,
'When they it think by Night conceal'd.   220
'Fly from their Vices. 'Tis thy state,
'Not Thee, that they would consecrate.
'Fly from their Ruine. How I fear
'Though guiltless lest thou perish there.'

What should he do? He would respect   225
Religion, but not Right neglect:
For first Religion taught him Right,
And dazled not but clear'd his sight.

Sometimes resolv'd his Sword he draws,
But reverenceth then the Laws: 230
For Justice still that Courage led;
First from a Judge, then Souldier bred.

XXX

Small Honour would be in the Storm.
The *Court* him grants the lawful Form;
Which licens'd either Peace or Force, 235
To hinder the unjust Divorce.
Yet still the *Nuns* his Right debar'd,
Standing upon their holy Guard.
Ill-counsell'd Women, do you know
Whom you resist, or what you do? 240

XXXI

Is not this he whose Offspring fierce
Shall fight through all the *Universe*;
And with successive Valour try
France, *Poland*, either *Germany*;
Till one, as long since prophecy'd, 245
His Horse through conquer'd *Britain* ride?
Yet, against Fate, his Spouse they kept;
And the great Race would intercept.

XXXII

Some to the Breach against their Foes
Their *Wooden Saints* in vain oppose. 250
Another bolder stands at push
With their old *Holy-Water Brush*.
While the disjointed *Abbess* threads
The gingling Chain-shot of her *Beads*.
But their lowd'st Cannon were their Lungs; 255
And sharpest Weapons were their Tongues.

87

But, waving these aside like Flyes,
Young *Fairfax* through the Wall does rise,
Then th' unfrequented Vault appear'd,
And superstitions vainly fear'd.   260
The *Relicks false* were set to view;
Only the Jewels there were true.
But truly bright and holy *Thwaites*
That weeping at the *Altar* waites.

But the glad Youth away her bears,   265
And to the *Nuns* bequeaths her Tears;
Who guiltily their Prize bemoan,
Like Gipsies that a Child hath stoln.
Thenceforth (as when th' Inchantment ends
The Castle vanishes or rends)   270
The wasting Cloister with the rest
Was in one instant dispossest.

XXXV

At the demolishing, this Seat
To *Fairfax* fell as by Escheat.
And what both *Nuns* and *Founders* will'd   275
'Tis likely better thus fulfill'd.
For if the *Virgin* prov'd not theirs,
The *Cloyster* yet remained hers.
Though many a *Nun* there made her Vow,
'Twas no *Religious House* till now.   280

From that blest Bed the *Heroe* came,
Whom *France* and *Poland* yet does fame:
Who, when retired here to Peace,
His warlike Studies could not cease;

But laid these Gardens out in sport   285
In the just Figure of a Fort;
And with five Bastions it did fence,
As aiming one for ev'ry Sense.

XXXVII

When in the *East* the Morning Ray
Hangs out the Colours of the Day,   290
The Bee through these known Allies hums,
Beating the *Dian* with its *Drumms*.
Then Flow'rs their drowsie Eylids raise,
Their Silken Ensigns each displayes,
And dries its Pan yet dank with Dew,   295
And fills its Flask with Odours new.

XXXVIII

These, as their *Governour* goes by,
In fragrant Vollyes they let fly;
And to salute their *Governess*
Again as great a charge they press: 300
None for the *Virgin Nymph*; for She
See ns with the Flow'rs a Flow'r to be.
And think so still! though not compare
With Breath so sweet, or Cheek so faire.

XXXIX

Well shot ye Firemen! Oh how sweet,   305
And round your equal Fires do meet;
Whose shrill report no Ear can tell,
But Ecchoes to the Eye and smell.
See how the Flow'rs, as at *Parade*,
Under their *Colours* stand displaid: 310
Each *Regiment* in order grows,
That of the Tulip Pinke and Rose.

XL

But when the vigilant *Patroul*
Of Stars walks round about the *Pole,*
Their Leaves, that to the stalks are curl'd,   315
Seem to their Staves the *Ensigns* furl'd.
Then in some Flow'rs beloved Hut
Each Bee as Sentinel is shut;
And sleeps so too: but, if once stir'd,
She runs you through, or askes *the Word.*   320

XLI

Oh Thou, that dear and happy Isle
The Garden of the World ere while,
Thou *Paradise* of four Seas,
Which *Heaven* planted us to please,
But, to exclude the World, did guard   325
With watry if not flaming Sword;
What luckless Apple did we tast,
To make us Mortal, and The Wast?

XLII

Unhappy! shall we never more
That sweet *Militia* restore,   330
When Gardens only had their Towrs,
And all the Garrisons were Flowrs,
When Roses only Arms might bear,
And Men did rosie Garlands wear?
Tulips, in several Colours barr'd,   335
Were then the *Switzers* of our *Guard.*

XLIII

The *Gardiner* had the *Souldiers* place,
And his more gentle Forts did trace.
The Nursery of all things green
Was then the only *Magazeen.*   340

The *Winter Quarters* were the Stoves,
Where he the tender Plants removes.
But War all this doth overgrow:
We Ord'nance Plant and Powder sow.

XLIV

And yet there walks one on the Sod   345
Who, had it pleased him and *God*,
Might once have made our Gardens spring
Fresh as his own and flourishing.
But he preferr'd to the *Cinque Ports*
These five imaginary Forts: 350
And, in those half-dry Trenches, spann'd
Pow'r which the Ocean might command.

XLV

For he did, with his utmost Skill,
Ambition weed, but *Conscience* till.
Conscience, that Heaven-nursed Plant,   355
Which most our Earthly Gardens want.
A prickling leaf it bears, and such
As that which shrinks at ev'ry touch;
But Flowrs eternal, and divine,
That in the Crowns of Saints do shine.   360

XLVI

The sight does from these *Bastions* ply,
Th' invisible *Artilery*;
And at proud *Cawood Castle* seems
To point the *Battery* of its Beams.
As if it quarrell'd in the Seat   365
Th' Ambition of its *Prelate* great.
But ore the Meads below it plays,
Or innocently seems to gaze.

XLVII

And now to the Abbyss I pass
Of that unfathomable Grass,   370
Where Men like Grashoppers appear,
But Grashoppers are Gyants there:
They, in their squeking Laugh, contemn
Us as we walk more low then them:
And, from the Precipices tall   375
Of the green spir's, to us do call.

XLVIII

To see Men through this Meadow Dive.
We wonder how they rise alive.
As, under Water, none does know
Whether he fall through it or go.   380
But, as the Marriners that sound.
And show upon their Lead the Ground,
They bring up Flow'rs so to be seen,
And prove they've at the Bottom been.

XLIX

No Scene that turns with Engines strange   385
Does oftner then these Meadows change.
For when the Sun the Grass hath vext,
The tawny Mowers enter next;
Who seem like *Israalites* to be,
Walking on foot through a green Sea.   390
To them the Grassy Deeps divine,
And crowd a Lane to either Side.

L

With whistling Sithe, and Elbow strong,
These Massacre the Grass along:
While one, unknowing, carves the *Rail*,   395
Whose yet unfeather'd Quils her fail.

The Edge all bloody from its Breast
He draws, and does his stroke detest;
Fearing the Flesh untimely mow'd
To him a Fate as black forebode.   400

LI

But bloody *Thestylis*, that waites
To bring the mowing Camp their Cates.
Greey as Kites has trust it up,
And forthwith means on it to sup:
When on another quick She lights,   405
And cryes, he call'd us *Israelites*;
But now, to make his saying trye,
Rails rain for Quails, for Manna Dew.

LII

Unhappy Birds! what does it boot
To build below the Grasses Root;   410
When Lowness is unsafe as Hight,
And Chance o'retakes what scapeth spight?
And now your Orphan Parents Call
Sounds your untimely Funeral.
Death-Trumpets creak in such a Note,   415
And 'tis the *Sourdine* in their Throat.

LIII

Or sooner hatch or higher build:
The Mower now commands the Field;
In whose new Traverse seemeth wrought
A Camp of Battail newly fought: 420
Where, as the Meads with Hay, the Plain
Lyes quilted ore with Bodies slain:
The Women that with forks it fling,
Do represent the Pillaging.

93

LIV

And now the careless Victors play,   425
Dancing the Triumphs of the Hay;
Where every Mowers wholesome Heat
Smells like an *Alexanders sweat*.
Their Females fragrant as the Mead
Which they in *Fairy Circles* tread: 430
When at their Dances End they kiss,
Their new-made Hay not sweeter is.

LV

When after this 'tis pil'd in Cocks,
Like a calm Sea it shews the Rocks:
We wondring in the River near   435
How Boats among them safely steer.
Or, like the *Desert Memphis Sand*,
Short *Pyramids* of Hay do stand.
And such the *Roman Camps* do rise
In Hills for Soldiers Obsequies.   440

LVI

This *Scene* again withdrawing brings
A new and empty Face of things;
A levell'd space, as smooth and plain,
As Clothes for *Lilly* strecht to stain.
The World when first created sure   445
Was such a Table rase and pure.
Or rather such is the *Toril*
Ere the Bulls enter at Madril.

LVII

For to this naked equal Flat,
Which *Levellers* take Pattern at,   450
The Villagers in common chase
Their Cattle, which it closer rase;

And what below the Sith increast
Is pincht yet nearer by the Beast.
Such, in the painted World, appear'd   455
Davenant with th' Universal Heard.

LVIII

They seem within the polisht Grass
A Landskip drawen in Looking-Glass.
And shrunk in the huge Pasture show
As Spots, so shap'd, on Faces do.   460
Such Fleas, ere they approach the Eye,
In Multiplying Glasses lye.
They feed so wide, so slowly move,
As *Constellations* do above.

LIX

Then, to conclude these pleasant Acts,   465
Denton sets ope its *Cataracts*;
And makes the Meadow truly be
(What it but seem'd before) a Sea.
For, jealous of its *Lords* long stay,
It try's t'invite him thus away.   470
The River in it self is drown'd,
And Isl's th' astonish'd Cattle round.

LX

Let others tell the *Paradox*,
How Eels now bellow in the Ox;
How Horses at their Tails do kick,   475
Turn'd as they hang to Leeches quick;
How Boats can over Bridges sail;
And Fishes do the Stables scale.
How *Salmons* trespassing are found;
And Pikes are taken in the Pound.   480

LXI

But I, retiring from the Flood,
Take Sanctuary in the Wood;
And, while it lasts, my self imbark
In this yet green, yet growing Ark;
Where the first Carpenter might best   485
Fit Timber for his Keel have Prest.
And where all Creatures might have shares;
Although in Armies, not in Paires.

LXII

The double Wood of ancient Stocks
Link'd in so thick, an Union locks,   490
It like two *Pedigrees* appears,
On one hand *Fairfax*, th' other *Veres*:
Of whom though many fell in War,
Yet more to Heaven shooting are:
And, as they Natures Cradle deckt,   495
Will in green Age her Hearse expect.

LXIII

When first the Eye this Forrest sees
It seems indeed as *Wood* not *Trees*:
As if their Neighbourhood so old
To one great Trunk them all did mold.   500
There the huge Bulk takes place, as ment
To thrust up a *Fifth Element*;
And stretches still so closely wedg'd
As if the Night within were hedg'd.

LXIV

Dark all without it knits; within   505
It opens passable and thin;
And in as loose an order grows,
As the *Corinthean Porticoes*.

The arching Boughs unite between
The Columnes of the Temple green;   510
And underneath the winged Quires
Echo about their tuned Fires.

The *Nightingale* does here make choice
To sing the Tryals of her Voice.
Low Shrubs she sits in, and adorns   515
With Musick high the squatted Thorns.
But highest Oakes stoop down to hear,
And listning Elders prick the Ear.
The Thorn, lest it should hurt her, draws
Within the Skin its shrunken claws.   520

But I have for my Musick found
A Sadder, yet more pleasing Sound:
The *Stock-doves*, whose fair necks are grac'd
With Nuptial Rings their Ensigns chast;
Yet always, for some Cause unknown,   525
Sad pair unto the Elms they moan.
O why should such a Couple mourn,
That in so equal Flames do burn!

Then as I careless on the Bed
Of gelid *Straw-berryes* do tread,   530
And through the Hazles thick espy
The hatching *Thrastles* shining Eye;
The *Heron* from the Ashes top,
The eldest of its young lets drop,
As if it Stork-like did pretend   535
That *Tribute* to *its Lord* to send.

97

But most the *Hewel's* wonders are,
Who here has the *Holt-felsters* care.
He walks still upright from the Root,
Meas'ring the Timber with his Foot;   540
And all the way, to keep it clean,
Doth from the Bark the Wood-moths glean.
He, with his Beak, examines well
Which fit to stand and which to fell.

The good he numbers up, and hacks;   545
As if he mark'd them with the Ax.
But where he, tinkling with his Beak,
Does find the hollow Oak to speak,
That for his building he designs,
And through the tainted Side he mines.   550
Who could have thought the *tallest Oak*
Should fall by such a *feeble Strok'* !

Nor would it, had the Tree not fed
A *Tratior-worm*, within it bred.
(As first our *Flesh* corrupt within   555
Tempts impotent and bashful *Sin*.)
And yet that *Worm* triumphs not long,
But serves to feed the *Hewels young*.
While the Oake seems to fall content,
Viewing the Treason's Punishment.   560

Thus I, *easie Philosopher*,
Among the *Birds* and *Trees* confer:
And little now to make me, wants
Or of the *Fowles*, or of the *Plants*.

Give me but Wings as they, and I 565
Streight floting on the Air shall fly:
Or turn me but, and you shall see
I was but an inverted Tree.

LXXII

Already I begin to call
In their most learned Original: 570
And where I Language want, my Signs
The Bird upon the Bough divines;
And more attentive there doth sit
Then if She were with Lime-twigs knit.
No Leaf does tremble in the Wind 575
Which I returning cannot find.

LXXIII

Out of these scatter'd *Sibyls* Leaves
Strange *Prophecies* my Phancy weaves:
And in one History consumes,
Like *Mexique Paintings*, all the *Plumes*. 580
What *Rome, Greece, Palestine*, ere said
I in this light *Mosaick* read.
Thrice happy he who, not mistook,
Hath read in *Natures mystick Book*.

LXXIV

And see how Chance's better Wit 585
Could with a Mask my studies hit!
The Oak-Leaves me embroyder all,
Between which Caterpillars crawl:
And Ivy, with familiar trails,
Me licks, and clasps, and curles, and hales. 590
Under this *antick Cope* I move
Like some great *Prelate of the Grove*,

99

Then, languishing with ease, I toss
On Pallets swoln of Velvet Moss;
While the Wind, cooling through the Boughs,   595
Flatters with Air my panting Brows.
Thanks for my Rest ye *Mossy Banks*,
And unto you *cool Zephyr's* Thanks,
Who, as my Hair, my Thoughts too shed,
And winnow from the Chaff my Head.   600

LXXVI

How safe, methinks, and strong, behind
These Trees have I incamp'd my Mind;
Where Beauty, aiming at the Heart,
Bends in some Tree its useless Dart;
And where the World no certain Shot   605
Can make, or me it toucheth not.
But I on it securely play,
And gaul its Horsemen all the Day.

LXXVII

Bind me ye *Woodbines* in your 'twines,
Curle me about ye gadding *Vines*,   610
And Oh so close your Circles lace,
That I may never leave this Place:
But, lest your Fetters prove too weak,
Ere I your Silken Bondage break,
Do you, *O Brambles*, chain me too,   615
And courteous *Briars* nail me through.

LXXVIII

Here in the Morning tye my Chain,
Where the two Woods have made a Lane:
While, like a *Guard* on either side,
The Trees before their *Lord* divide;   620

This, like a long and equal Thread,
Betwixt two *Labyrinths* does lead.
But, where the Floods did lately drown,
There at the Ev'ning stake me down.

LXXIX

For now the Waves are fal'n and dry'd,   625
And now the Meadows fresher dy'd;
Whose Grass, with moister colour dasht,
Seems as green Silks but newly washt.
No *Serpent* new nor *Crocodile*
Remains behind our little *Nile*;   630
Unless it self you will mistake,
Among these Meads the only Snake.

LXXX

See in what wanton harmless folds
It ev'ry where the Meadow holds;
And its yet muddy back doth lick,   635
Till as a *Chrystal Mirrour* slick;
Where all things gaze themselves, and doubt
If they be it or without.
And for his shade which therein shines,
Narcissus like, the *Sun* too pines.   640

LXXXI

Oh what a Pleasure 'tis to hedge
My Temples here with heavy sedge;
Abandoning my lazy Side,
Strecht as a Bank unto the Tide;
Or to suspend my sliding Foot   645
On the Osiers undermined Root,
And in its Branches tough to hang,
While at my Lines the Fishes twang!

But now away my Hooks, my Quills,
And Angles, idle Utensils.   650
The *young Maria* walks to night:
Hide trifling Youth thy Pleasures slight.
'Twere shame that such judicious Eyes
Should with such Toyes a Man surprize;
She that already is the *Law*   655
Of all her *Sex*, her *Ages Aw*.

See how loose Nature, in respect
To her, it self doth recollect;
And every thing so whisht and fine,
Starts forth with to its *Bonne Mine*.   660
The *Sun* himself, of *Her* aware,
Seems to descend with greater Care;
And lest *She* see him go to Bed,
In blushing Clouds conceales his Head.

So when the Shadows laid asleep   665
From underneath these Banks do creep,
And on the River as it flows
With *Eben Shuts* begin to close;
The modest *Halcyon* comes in sight,
Flying betwixt the Day and Night;   670
And such an horror calm and dumb,
Admiring Nature does benum.

The viscous Air, wheres'ere She fly,
Follows and sucks her Azure dy;
The gellying Stream compacts below,   675
If it might fix her shadow so ;

The stupid Fishes hang, as plain
As *Flies* in *Chrystal* overt'ane;
And Men the silent *Scene* assist,
Charm'd with the *Saphir-winged Mist*.   680

LXXXVI

Maria such, and so doth hush
The *World*, and through the *Ev'ning* rush.
No new-born *Comet* such a Train
Draws through the Skie, nor Star new-slain.
For streight those giddy Rockets fail,   685
Which from the putrid Earth exhale,
But by her *Flames*, in *Heaven* try'd,
Nature is wholly *vitrifi'd*.

LXXXVII

'Tis *She* that to these Gardens gave
That wondrous Beauty which they have;   690
She streightness on the Woods bestows;
To *Her* the Meadow sweetness owes;
Nothing could make the River be
So Chrystal-pure but only *She*;
She yet more Pure, Sweet, Streight, and Fair,   695
Then Gardens, Woods, Meads, Rivers are.

LXXXVIII

Therefore what first *She* on them spent,
They gratefully again present.
The Meadow Carpets where to tread;
The Garden Flow'rs to Crown *Her* Head;   700
And for a Glass the limpid Brook,
Where *She* may all *her* Beautyes look;
But, since *She* would not have them seen,
The Wood about *her* draws a Skreen.

For *She*, to higher Beauties rais'd,   705
Disdains to be for lesser prais'd.
She counts her Beauty to converse
In all the Languages as *hers*;
Nor yet in those *her self* imployes
But for the *Wisdome*, not the *Noyse*;   710
Nor yet that *Wisdome* would affect,
But as 'tis *Heavens Dialect*.

LXXXX

Blest Nymph! that couldst so soon prevent
Those *Trains* by Youth against thee meant;
Tears (watry Shot that pierce the Mind;)   715
And *Sighs* (Loves Cannon charg'd with Wind;)
True Praise (That breaks through all defence;)
And *feign'd complying Innocence*;
But knowing where this *Ambush* lay,
She scap'd the safe, but roughest Way.   720

LXXXXI

This 'tis to have been from the first
In a *Domestick Heaven* nurst,
Under the *Discipline* severe
Of *Fairfax* and the starry *Vere*;
Where not one object can come nigh   725
But pure, and spotless as the Eye;
And *Goodness* doth it self intail
On *Females*, if there want a *Male*.

LXXXXII

Go now fond Sex that on your Face
Do all your useless Study place,   730
Nor once at Vice your Brows dare knit
Lest the smooth Forehead wrinkled sit:

Yet your own Face shall at you grin,
Thorough the Black-bag of your Skin;
When *knowledge* only could have fill'd   735
And *Virtue* all those *Furrows* till'd.

LXXXXIII

Hence *She* with Graces more divine
Supplies beyond her *Sex* the *Line*;
And, like a *sprig of Misleto*,
On the *Fairfacian Oak* does grow;   740
Whence, for some universal good,
The *Priest* shall cut the sacred Bud;
While her *glad Parents* most rejoice,
And make their *Destiny* their *Choice*.

LXXXXIV

Mean time ye Fields, Springs, Bushes, Flow'rs,   745
Where yet She leads her studious Hours,
(Till Fate her worthily translates,
And find a *Fairfax* for our *Thwaites*)
Employ the means you have by Her,
And in your kind your selves preferr;   750
That, as all *Virgins* She preceds,
So you all *Woods, Streams, Gardens, Meads*.

LXXXXV

For you *Thessalian Tempe's Seat*
Shall now be scorn'd as obsolete;
Aranjuez, as less, disdain'd;   755
The *Bel-Retiro* as constrain'd;
But name not the *Idalian Grove*,
For 'twas the Seat of wanton Love;
Much less the Dead's *Elysian Fields*,
Yet nor to them your Beauty yields.   760

'Tis not, what once it was, the *World*:
But a rude heap together hurl'd;
All negligently overthrown,
Gulfes, Deserts, Precipices, Stone.
Your lesser *World* contains the same.   765
But in more decent Order tame;
You Heaven's Center, Nature's Lap.
And Paradice's only Map.

But now the *Salmon-Fisher's* moist
Their *Leathern Boats* begin to hoist;   770
And, like *Antipodes* in Shoes,
Have shod their *Heads* in their *Canoos.*
How *Tortoise* like, but not so slow,
These rational *Amphibii* go?
Let's in: for the dark *Hemisphere*   775
Does now like one of them appear.

On the Victory obtained by Blake over the Spaniards in the Bay of Sanctacruze, in the Island of Teneriff, 1657

Now does *Spains* Fleet her spatious wings unfold,
Leaves the new World and hastens for the old:
But though the wind was fair, they slowly swoome
Frayted with acted Guilt, and Guilt to come:
For this rich load, of which so proud they are,   5
Was rais'd by Tyranny, and rais'd for War;
Every capatious Gallions womb was fill'd,

With what the Womb of wealthy Kingdomes yield,
The new Worlds wounded Intrails they had tore,
For wealth wherewith to wound the old once more.   10
Wealth which all others Avarice might cloy,
But yet in them caus'd as much fear, as Joy.
For now upon the Main, themselves they saw,
That boundless Empire, where you give the Law,
Of winds and waters rage, they fearful be,   15
But much more fearful are your Flags to see.
Day, that to those who sail upon the deep,
More wish't for, and more welcome is then sleep,
They dreaded to behold, Least the Sun's light,
With *English* Streamers, should salute their sight: 20
In thickest darkness they would choose to steer,
So that such darkness might suppress their fear;
At length theirs vanishes, and fortune smiles;
For they behold the sweet Canary Isles;
One of which doubtless is by Nature blest   25
Above both Worlds, since 'tis above the rest.
For least some Gloominess might stain her sky,
Trees there the duty of the Clouds supply;
O noble Trust which Heaven on this Isle poures,
Fertile to be, yet never need her showres.   30
A happy Peop!e, which at once do gain
The benefits without the ills of rain.
Both health and profit Fate cannot deny;
Where still the Earth is moist, the Air still dry:
The jarring Elements no discord know,   35
Fewel and Rain together kindly grow;
And coolness there, with heat doth never fight,
This only rules by day, and that by Night.
Your worth to all these Isles, a just right brings,
The best of Lands should have the best of Kings.   40
And these want nothing Heaven can afford,
Unless it be, the having you their Lord;

But this great want, will not a long one prove,
Your Conquering Sword will soon that want remove.
For *Spain* had better, Shee'l ere long confess,   45
Have broken all her Swords, then this one Peace,
Casting that League off, which she held so long,
She cast off that which only made her strong.
Forces and art, she soon will feel, are vain,
Peace, against you, was the sole strength of *Spain*.   50
By that alone those Islands she secures,
Peace made them hers, but War will make them yours
There the indulgent Soil that rich Grape breeds,
Which of the Gods the fancied drink exceeds;
They still do yield, such is their pretious mould,   55
All that is good, and are not curst with Gold.
With fatal Gold, for still where that does grow,
Neither the Soyl, nor People quiet know.
Which troubles men to raise it when 'tis Oar,
And when 'tis raised, does trouble them much more.   60
Ah, why was thither brought that cause of War,
Kind Nature had from thence remov'd so far.
In vain doth she those Islands free from Ill,
If fortune can make guilty what she will.
But whilst I draw that Scene, where you ere long,   65
Shalll conquests act, your present are unsung,
    For *Sanctacruze* the glad Fleet takes her way.
And safely there casts Anchor in the Bay.
Never so many with one joyful cry,
That place saluted, where they all must dye.   70
Deluded men! Fate with you did but sport,
You scap't the Sea, to perish in your Port.
'Twas more for *Englands* fame you should dye there,
Where you had most of strength, and least of fear.
    The Peek's proud height, the *Spaniards* all admire,   75
Yet in their brests, carry a pride much higher.
Onely to this vast hill a power is given,

108

At once both to Inhabit Earth and Heaven.
But this stupendious Prospect did not neer,
Make them admire, so much as they did fear.   80
    For here they met with news, which did produce,
A grief, above the cure of Grapes best juice.
They learn'd with Terrour, that nor Summers heat,
Nor Winters storms, had made your Fleet retreat.
To fight against such Foes, was vain they knew,   85
Which did the rage of Elements subdue.
Who on the Ocean that does horror give,
To all besides, triumphantly do live.
    With hast they therefore all their Gallions moar,
And flank with Cannon from the Neighbouring shore.   90
Forts, Lines, and Sconces all the Bay along,
They build and act all that can make them strong.
    Fond men who know not whilst such works they raise,
They only Labour to exalt your praise.
Yet they by restless toyl, became at Length,   95
So proud and confident of their made strength.
That they with joy their boasting General heard,
Wish then for that assault he lately fear'd.
His wish he has, for now undaunted *Blake*,
With winged speed, for *Sanctacruze* does make.   100
For your renown, his conquering Fleet does ride,
Ore Seas as vast as is the *Spaniards* pride.
Whose Fleet and Trenches view'd, he soon did say,
We to their Strength are more oblig'd then they.
Were't not for that, they from their Fate would run, 105
And a third World seek out our Armes to shun.
Those Forts, which there, so high and strong appear
Do not so much suppress, as shew their fear.
Of Speedy Victory let no man doubt,
Our worst works past, now we have found them out.   110
Behold their Navy does at Anchor lye,
And they are ours, for now they cannot fly.

This said, the whole Fleet gave it their applause,
And all assumes your courage, in your cause.
That Bay they enter, which unto them owes,   115
The noblest wreaths, that Victory bestows.
Bold *Stainer* Leads, this Fleets design'd by fate.
To give him Lawrel, as the Last did Plate.

The Thund'ring Cannon now begins the Fight,
And though it be at Noon, creates a Night.   120
The Air was soon after the fight begun,
Far more enflam'd by it, then by the Sun.
Never so burning was that Climate known,
War turn'd the temperate, to the Torrid Zone.

Fate these two Fleets, between both Worlds had brought   125
Who fight, as if for both those Worlds they fought.
Thousands of wayes, Thousands of men there dye,
Some Ships are sunk, some blown up in the skie.
Nature never made Cedars so high a Spire,
As Oakes did then, Urg'd by the active fire.   130
Which by quick powders force, so high was sent,
That it return'd to its own Element.
Torn Limbs some leagues into the Island fly,
Whilst others lower, in the Sea do lye.
Scarce souls from bodies sever'd are so far,   135
By death, as bodies there were by the War.
Th' all-seeing Sun, neer gaz'd on such a sight,
Two dreadful Navies there at Anchor Fight.
And neither have, or power, or will to fly,
There one must Conquer, or there both must dye.   140
Far different Motives yet, engag'd them thus,
Necessity did them, but Choice did us.

A choice which did the highest worth express,
And was attended by as high success.
For your resistless genious there did Raign,   145
By which we Laurels reapt ev'n on the Mayn
So prosperous Stars, though absent to the sence,

Bless those they shine for, by their Influence.
  Our Cannon now tears every Ship and Sconce,
And o're two Elements Triumphs at once.   150
Their Gallions sunk, their wealth the Sea does fill,
The only place where it can cause no Ill.
  Ah would those Treasures which both Indies have,
Were buryed in as large, and deep a grave,
Wars chief support with them would buried be,   155
And the Land owe her peace unto the Sea.
  Ages to come, your conquering Arms will bless,
There they destroy, what had destroy'd their Peace.
And in one War the present age may boast,
That certain seeds of many Wars are lost.   160
  All the Foes Ships destroy'd, by Sea or fire,
Victorious *Blake*, does from the Bay retire,
His seige of *Spain* he then again pursues,
And there first brings of his success the news;
The saddest news that ere to *Spain* was brought,   165
Their rich Fleet sunk, and ours with Lawrel fraught.
Whilst fame in every place, her Trumpet blowes,
And tells the World, how much to you it owes.

A Dialogue between Thyrsis and Dorinda

Dorinda. WHEN Death, shall snatch us from these Kids,
            And shut up our divided Lids,
            Tell me, *Thyrsis*, prethee do,
            Whither thou and I must go.

Thyrsis. To the Elizium: (*Dorinda*) oh where i'st?   5
Thyrsis. A Chast Soul, can never mis't.
Dorinda. I know no way, but one, our home;
            Is our cell Elizium?

Thyrsis. Cast thine Eye to yonder Skie,
       There the milky way doth lye;   10
       'Tis a sure but rugged way,
       That leads to Everlasting day.

Dorinda. There Birds may nest, but how can I,
       That have no wings and cannot fly?

Thyrsis. Do not sigh (fair Nimph) for fire   15
       Hath no wings, yet doth aspire
       Till it hit, against the pole,
       Heaven's the Centre of the Soul.

Dorinda. But in Elizium how do they
       Pass Eternity away?   20

Thyrsis. Ho, ther's, neither hope nor fear
       Ther's no Wolf, no Fox, nor Bear.
       No need of Dog to fetch our stray,
       Our Lightfoot we may give away;
       No Oat-pipe's needfull, there thine Ears   25
       May feast with Musick of the Spheres.

Dorinda. Oh sweet! oh sweet! How I my future state
       By silent thinking, Antidate:
       I prethee let us spend, our time to come,
       In talking of *Elizium*.

Thyrsis. Then I'le go on: There, sheep are full   30
       Of softest grass, and softest wooll;
       There, birds sing Consorts, garlands grow,
       Cool winds do whisper, springs do flow.
       There, alwayes is, a rising Sun,   35
       And day is ever, but begun.
       Shepheards there, bear equal sway,
       And every Nimph's a Queen of *May*.

Dorinda. Ah me, ah me. *Thyrsis. Dorinda,* why do'st Cry?

Dorinda. I'm sick, I'm sick, and fain would dye: 40
　　　　Convinc' me now, that this is true;
　　　　By bidding, with mee, all adieu.

Thyrsis. I cannot live, without thee, I
　　　　Will for thee, much more with thee dye.

CHORUS. Then let us give *Carillo* charge o'th Sheep,   45
　　　　And thou and I'le pick poppies and them steep
　　　　In wine, and drink on't even till we weep,
　　　　So shall we smoothly pass away in sleep.

The Character of Holland

HOLLAND that scarce deserves the name of *Land,*
As but th' Off-scouring of the *British Sand;*
And so much Earth as was contributed
By *English Pilots* when they heav'd the Lead;
Or what by th' Oceans slow alluvion fell,   5
Of shipwrackt Cockle and the Muscle-shell;
This indigested vomit of the Sea
Fell to the *Dutch* by just Propriety.
　Glad then, as Miners that have found the Oar,
They with mad labour fish'd the *Land* to *Shoar;*   10
And div'd as desperately for each piece
Of Earth, as if't had been of *Ambergreece;*
Collecting anxiously small Loads of Clay,
Less then what building Swallows bear away;
Or then those Pills which sordid Beetles roul,   15
Transfusing into them their Dunghil Soul.

How did they rivet, with Gigantick Piles,
Thorough the Center their new-catched Miles;
And to the stake a strugling Country bound,
Where barking Waves still bait the forced Ground;   20
Building their *watry Babel* far more high
To reach the *Sea*, then those to scale the *Sky*.
  Yet still his claim the Injur'd Ocean laid,
And oft at Leap-frog ore their Steeples plaid:
As if on purpose it on Land had come   25
To shew them what's their *Mare Liberum*.
A daily deluge over them does boyl;
The Earth and Water play at *Level-coyl*;
The Fish oft-times the Burger dispossest,
And sat not as a Meat but as a Guest;   30
And oft the *Tritons* and the *Sea-Nymphs* saw
Whole sholes of *Dutch* serv'd up for *Cabillau*;
Or as they over the new Level rang'd
For pickled *Herring*, pickled *Heeren* chang'd.
Nature, it seem'd, asham'd of her mistake,   35
Would throw their Land away at *Duck* and *Drake*.
  Therefore *Necessity*, that first made *Kings*,
Something like *Government* among them brings.
For as with *Pygmees* who best kills the *Crane*,
Among the *hungry* he that treasures *Grain*,   40
Among the *blind* the one-ey'd *blinkard* reigns,
So rules among the *drowned* he that *draines*.
Not who first see the *rising Sun* commands,
But who could first discern the *rising Lands*.
Who best could know to pump an Earth so leak   45
Him they their *Lord* and *Country's Father* speak.
To make a *Bank* was a great *Plot of State*;
Invent a *Shov'l* and be a *Magistrate*.
Hence some small *Dyke-grave* unperceiv'd invades
The *Pow'r*, and grows as 'twere a *King of Spades*.   50
But for less envy some *joynt States* endures,

Who look like a *Commission of the Sewers*.
For these *Half-anders*, half wet, and half dry,
Nor bear *strict service*, nor *pure Liberty*.
　'Tis probable *Religion* after this   55
Came next in order; which they could not miss.
How could the *Dutch* but be converted, when
Th' *Apostles* were so many Fishermen?
Besides the Waters of themselves did rise,
And, as their Land, so them did re-baptize.   60
Though *Herring* for their *God* few voices mist,
And *Poor-John* to have been th' *Evangelist*.
Faith, that could never Twins conceive before,
Never so fertile, spawn'd upon this shore:
More pregnant then their *Marg'ret*, that laid down   65
For *Hans-in-Kelder* of a whole *Hans-Town*.
　Sure when *Religion* did it self imbark,
And from the *East* would *Westward* steer its Ark,
It struck, and splitting on this unknown ground,
Each one thence pillag'd the first piece he found: 70
Hence *Amsterdam*, *Turk-Christian-Pagan-Jew*,
Staple of Sects and Mint of Schisme grew;
That *Bank of Conscience*, where not one so strange
Opinion but finds Credit, and Exchange.
In vain for *Catholicks* our selves we bear;   75
The *universal Church* is onely there.
Nor can Civility there want for *Tillage*,
Where wisely for their *Court* they chose a *Village*.
How fit a Title clothes their *Governours*,
Themselves the *Hogs* as all their Subjects *Bores*!   80
　Let it suffice to give their Country Fame
That it had one *Civilis* call'd by Name,
Some Fifteen hundred and more years ago;
But surely never any that was so.
　See but their *Mairmaids* with their *Tails of Fish*,   85
Reeking at *Church* over the *Chafing-Dish*.

A vestal Turf enshrin'd in Earthen Ware
Fumes through the loop-holes of a wooden Square.
Each to the *Temple* with these *Altars* tend,
But still does place it at her *Western End*:   90
While the fat steam of *Female Sacrifice*
Fills the *Priests Nostrils* and puts out his *Eyes*.

Or what a Spectacle the *Skipper gross*,
A *Water-Hercules Butter-Coloss*,
Tunn'd up with all their sev'ral *Towns of Beer*;   95
When Stagg'ring upon some Land, *Snick and Sneer*,
They try, like Statuaries, if they can,
Cut out each others *Athos* to a Man:
And carve in their large Bodies, where they please,
The Armes of the *United Provinces*.   100

But when such Amity at home is show'd;
What then are their confederacies abroad?
Let this one court'sie witness all the rest;
When their whole Navy they together prest,
Not Christian Captives to redeem from Bands: 105
Or intercept the Western golden Sands:
No, but all ancient Rights and Leagues must vail.
Rather then to the *English* strike their sail;
To whom their weather-beaten *Province* ows
It self, when as some greater Vessel tows   110
A Cock-boat tost with the same wind and fate;
We buoy'd so often up their *sinking State*.

Was this *Jus Belli & Pacis*; could this be
Cause why their *Burgomaster of the Sea*
Ram'd with Gun-powder, flaming with Brand wine,   115
Should raging hold his Linstock to the Mine?
While, with feign'd *Treaties*, they invade by stealth
Our sore new circumcised *Common wealth*.

Yet of his vain Attempt no more he sees
Then of *Case-Butter* shot and *Bullet-Cheese*.   120
And the torn Navy stagger'd with him home,

116

While the Sea laught it self into a foam,
'Tis true since that (as fortune kindly sports,)
A wholesome Danger drove us to our Ports.
While half their banish'd keels the Tempest tost,   125
Half bound at home in Prison to the frost:
That ours mean time at leizure might careen,
In a calm Winter, under Skies Serene.
As the obsequious Air and Waters rest,
Till the dear *Halcyon* hatch out all its nest.   130
The *Common wealth* doth by its losses grow;
And, like its own Seas, only Ebbs to flow.
Besides that very Agitation laves,
And purges out the corruptible waves.
    And now again our armed *Bucentore*   135
Doth yearly their *Sea-Nuptials* restore.
And now the *Hydra of seaven Provinces*
Is strangled by our *Infant Hercules.*
Their Tortoise wants its vainly stretched neck;
Their Navy all our Conquest or our Wreck: 140
Or, what is left, their *Carthage* overcome
Would render fain unto our better *Rome.*
Unless our *Senate*, lest their Youth disuse,
The War (but who would) Peace if begg'd refuse.
    For now of nothing may our *State* despair,   145
Darling of Heaven, and of Men the Care;
Provided that they be what they have been,
Watchful abroad, and honest still within.
For while our *Neptune* doth a *Trident* shake,
Steel'd with those piercing Heads, *Dean, Monck* and *Blake*,   150
And while *Jove* governs in the highest Sphere,
Vainly in *Hell* let *Pluto* domineer.

An Horatian Ode upon Cromwel's Return from Ireland

THE forward Youth that would appear
Must now forsake his *Muses* dear,
    Nor in the Shadows sing
    His Numbers languishing.
'Tis time to leave the Books in dust,   5
And oyl th' unused Armours rust,
    Removing from the Wall
    The Corslet of the Hall.
So restless *Cromwel* could not cease
In the inglorious Arts of Peace,   10
    But through adventrous War
    Urged his active Star.
And, like three fork'd Lightning, first
Breaking the Clouds where it was nurst,
    Did through his own Side   15
    His fiery way divide.
For 'tis all one to Courage high
The Emulous or Enemy;
    And with such to inclose
    Is more then to oppose.   20
Then burning through the Air he went,
And Pallaces and Templas rent:
    And *Cæsars* head at last
    Did through his Laurels blast.
'Tis Madness to resist or blame   25
The force of angry Heavens flame:
    And, if we would speak true,
    Much to the Man is due.

Who, from his private Gardens, where
He liv'd reserved and austere,   30
    As if his highest plot
    To plant the Bergamot,
Could by industrious Valour climbe
To ruine the great Work of Time,
    And cast the Kingdome old   35
    Into another Mold.
Though Justice against Fate complain,
And plead the antient Rights in vain:
    But those do hold or break
    As Men are strong or weak.   40
Nature that hateth emptiness,
Allows of penetration less:
    And therefore must make room
    Where greater Spirits come.
What Field of all the Civil Wars,   45
Where his were not the deepest Scars?
    And *Hampton* shows what part
    He had of wiser Art.
Where, twining subtile fears with hope,
He wove a Net of such a scope,   50
    That *Charles* himself might chase
    To *Caresbrooks* narrow case.
That thence the *Royal Actor* born
The *Tragick Scaffold* might adorn:
    While round the armed Bands   55
    Did clap their bloody hands.
He nothing common did or mean
Upon that memorable Scene:
    But with his keener Eye
    The Axes edge did try: 60
Nor call'd the *Gods* with vulgar spight
To vindicate his helpless Right,
    But bow'd his comely Head,

Down as upon a Bed.
This was that memorable Hour   65
Which first assur'd the forced Pow'r.
    So when they did design
    The *Capitols* first Line,
A bleeding Head where they begun,
Did fright the Architects to run;   70
    And yet in that the *State*
    Foresaw it's happy Fate.
And now the *Irish* are asham'd
To see themselves in one Year tam'd.
    So much one Man can do,   75
    That does both act and know.
They can affirm his Praises best,
And have, though overcome, confest
    How good he is, how just,
    And fit for highest Trust: 80
Nor yet grown stiffer with Command,
But still in the *Republick's* hand:
    How fit he is to sway
    That can so well obey.

He to the *Commons Feet* presents   85
A *Kingdome*, for his first years rents:
    And, what he may, forbears
    His Fame to make it theirs:
And has his Sword and Spoyls ungirt,
To lay them at the *Publick's* skirt.   90
    So when the Falcon high
    Falls heavy from the Sky,
She, having kill'd, no more does search,
But on the next green Bow to pearch;
    Where, when he first does lure,   95
    The Falckner has her sure.
What may not then our *Isle* presume
While Victory his Crest does plume!

What may not others fear
If thus he crown each Year!   100
A *Cæsar* he ere long to *Gaul*,
To *Italy* an *Hannibal*,
    And to all States not free
    Shall *Clymacterick* be.
The *Pict* no shelter now shall find   105
Within his party-colour'd Mind;
    But from this Valour sad
    Shrink underneath the Plad:
Happy if in the tufted brake
The *English Hunter* him mistake;   110
    Nor lay his Hounds in near
    The *Caledonian* Deer.
But thou the Wars and Fortunes Son
March indefatigably on:
    And for the last effect   115
    Still keep thy Sword erect;
Besides the force it has to fright
The Spirits of the shady Night,
    The same *Arts* that did *gain*
    A *Pow'r* must it *maintain*.   120

The First Anniversary of the Government under O.C.

LIKE the vain Curlings of the Watry maze,
Which in smooth streams a sinking Weight does raise:
So Man, declining alwayes, disappears
In the weak Circles of increasing Years;
And his short Tumults of themselves Compose,
While flowing Time above his Head does close.

Cromwell alone with greater Vigour runs,
(Sun-like) the Stages of succeeding Suns:
And still the Day which he doth next restore,
Is the just Wonder of the Day before.   10
Cromwell alone doth with new Lustre spring,
And shines the Jewel of the yearly Ring.
'Tis he the force of scattered Time contracts,
And in one Year the work of Ages acts:
While heavy Monarchs make a wide Return,   15
Longer, and more Malignant then *Saturn*:
And though they all *Platonique* years should raign
In the same Posture would be found again.
Their earthy Projects under ground they lay,
More slow and brittle then the *China* clay: 20
Well may they strive to leave them to their Son,
For one Thing never was by one King don.
Yet some more active for a Frontier Town
Took in by Proxie, beggs a false Renown;
Another triumphs at the publick Cost,   25
And will have Wonn, if he no more have Lost;
They fight by Others, but in Person wrong,
And only are against their Subjects strong;
Their other Wars seem but a feign'd contest,
This Common Enemy is still opprest;   30
If Conquerors, on them they turn their might;
If Conquered, on them they wreak their Spight:
They neither build the Temple in their dayes,
Nor Matter for succeeding Founders raise;
Nor sacred Prophecies consult within,   35
Much less themselves to perfect them begin;
No other care they bear of things above,
But with Astrologers, divine, and *Jove*,
To know how long their Planet yet Reprives
From the deserved Fate their guilty lives: 40
Thus (Image-like) an useless time they tell,

And with vain Scepter strike the hourly Bell;
Nor more contribute to the state of Things,
Then wooden Heads unto the Viols strings.
    While indefatigable *Cromwell* hyes, 45
And cuts his way still nearer to the Skyes,
Learning a Musique in the Region clear,
To tune this lower to that higher Sphere.
    So when *Amphion* did the Lute command,
Which the God gave him; with his gentle hand, 50
    The rougher Stones, unto his Measures hew'd,
Dans'd up in order from the Quarreys rude;
This took a Lower, that an Higher place,
As he the Treble alter'd, or the Base:
No Note he struck, but a new Story lay'd, 55
And the great Work ascended while he play'd.
    The listning Structures he with Wonder ey'd,
And still new Stopps to various Time apply'd:
Now through the Strings a Martial rage he throws,
And joying streight the *Theban* Tow'r arose; 60
Then as he strokes them with a Touch more sweet,
The flocking Marbles in a Palace meet;
But, for he most the graver Notes did try,
Therefore the Temples rear'd their Columns high:
Thus, ere he ceas'd, his sacred Lute creates 65
Th' harmonious City of the seven Gates.
    Such was that wondrous Order and Consent,
When *Cromwell* tun'd the ruling Instrument;
While tedious Statesmen many years did hack,
Framing a Liberty that still went back; 70
Whose num'rous Gorge could swallow in an hour
That Island, which the Sea cannot devour:
Then our *Amphion* issues out and sings,
And once he struck, and twice, the pow'rful Strings.
    The Commonwealth then first together came, 75
And each one enter'd in the willing Frame;

All otheMatter yields, and may be rul'd;
But who the Minds of stubborn Men can build?
No Quarry bears a Stone so hardly wrought,
Nor with such labour from its Center brought;   80
None to be sunk in the Foundation bends,
Each in the House the highest Place contends,
And each the Hand that lays him will direct,
And some fall back upon the Architect;
Yet all compos'd by his attractive Song,   85
Into the Animated City throng.

  The Common-wealth does through their Centers all
Draw the Circumf'rence of the publique Wall;
The crossest Spirits here do take their part,
Fast'ning the Contignation which they thwart;   90
And they, whose Nature leads them to divide,
Uphold, this one, and that the other Side;
But the most Equal still sustein the Height,
And they as Pillars keep the Work upright;
While the resistance of opposed Minds,   95
The Fabrick as with Arches stronger binds,
Which on the Basis of a Senate free,
Knit by the Roofs Protecting weight agree.

  When for his Foot he thus a place had found,
He hurles e'er since the World about him round;   100
And in his sev'ral Aspects, like a Star,
Here shines in Peace, and thither shoots a War.
While by his Beams observing Princes steer,
And wisely court the Influence they fear;
O would they rather by his Pattern won.   105
Kiss the approaching, nor yet angry Son;
And in their numbred Footsteps humbly tread
The path where holy Oracles do lead;
How might they under such a Captain raise,
The great Designes kept for the latter Dayes!   110
But mad with Reason, so miscall'd, of State

They know them not, and what they know not, hate,
Hence still they sing Hosanna to the Whore,
And her whom they should Massacre adore:
But Indians whom they should convert, subdue;   115
Nor teach, but traffique with, or burn the Jew.
  Unhappy Princes, ignorantly bred,
By Malice some, by Errour more misled;
If gracious Heaven to my Life give length,
Leisure to Time, and to my Weakness Strength,   120
Then shall I once with graver Accents shake
Your Regal sloth, and your long Slumbers wake;
Like the shrill Huntsman that prevents the East,
Winding his Horn to Kings that chase the Beast.
  Till then my Muse shall hollow far behind   125
Angelique *Cromwell* who outwings the wind;
And in dark Nights and in cold Dayes alone
Pursues the Monster thorough every Throne:
Which shrinking to her *Roman* Den impure,
Gnashes her Goary teeth; nor there secure.   130
  Hence oft I think, if in some happy Hour
High Grace should meet in one with highest Pow'r,
And then a seasonable People still
Should bend to his, as he to Heavens will,
What we might hope, what wonderful Effect   135
From such a wish'd Conjuncture might reflect.
Sure, the mysterious Work, where none withstand,
Would forthwith finish under such a Hand:
Fore-shortned Time its useless Course would stay,
And soon precipitate the latest Day.   140
But a thick Cloud about that Morning lyes,
And intercepts the Beams of Mortal eyes,
That 'tis the most which we determine can,
If these the Times, then this must be the Man.
And well he therefore does, and well has guest,   145
Who in his Age has always forward prest:

And knowing not where Heaven's choice may light,
Girds yet his Sword, and ready stands to fight;
But Men alas, as if they nothing car'd,
Look on, all unconcern'd, or unprepar'd;   150
And Stars still fall, and still the Dragons Tail
Swinges the Volumes of its horrid Flail.
For the great Justice that did first suspend
The World by Sin, does by the same extend.
Hence that blest Day still counterpoysed wastes,   155
The Ill delaying, what th' Elected hastes;
Hence landing Nature to new Seas is tost,
And good Designes still with their Authors lost.
    And thou, great *Cromwell*, for whose happy birth
A Mold was chosen out of better Earth;   160
Whose Saint-like Mother we did lately see
Live out an Age, long as a Pedigree;
That she might seem, could we see the Fall dispute,
T' have smelt the Blossome, and not eat the Fruit;
Though none does of more lasting Parents grow,   165
But never any did them Honor so;
Though thou thine Heart from Evil still unstain'd,
And always hast thy Tongue from fraud refrain'd;
Thou, who so oft through Storms of thundring Lead
Hast born securely thine undaunted Head,   170
Thy Brest through ponyarding Conspiracies,
Drawn from the Sheath of lying Prophecies;
Thee proof beyond all other Force or Skill,
Our Sins endanger, and shall one day kill.
    How near they fail'd, and in thy sudden Fall   175
At once assay'd to overturn us all.
Our brutish fury strugling to be Free,
Hurry'd thy Horses while they hurry'd thee.
When thou hadst almost quit thy Mortal cares,
And soyl'd in Dust thy Crown of silver Hairs.   180
Let this one Sorrow interweave among

126

The other Glories of our yearly Song.
Like skilful Looms which through the costly threed
Of purling Ore, a shining wave do shed:
So shall the Tears we on past Grief employ,   185
Still as they trickle, glitter in our Joy.
So with more Modesty we may be True,
And speak as of the Dead the Praises due:
While impious Men deceiv'd with pleasure short,
On their own Hopes shall find the Fall retort.   190
But the poor Beasts wanting their noble Guide,
What could they more? shrunk guiltily aside.
First winged Fear transports them far away,
And leaden Sorrow then their flight did stay.
See how they each his tow'ring Crest abate,   195
And the green Grass, and their known Mangers hate,
Nor through wide Nostrils snuffe the wanton air,
Nor their round Hoofs, or curled Mane's compare;
With wandring Eyes, and restless Ears they stood,
And with shrill Neighings ask'd him of the Wood.   200
Thou *Cromwell* falling, not a stupid Tree,
Or Rock so savage, but it mourn'd for thee:
And all about was heard a Panique groan,
As if that Nature's self were overthrown.
It seemed the Earth did from the Center tear;   205
It seemed the Sun was faln out of the Sphere:
Justice obstructed lay, and Reason fool'd;
Courage disheartened, and Religion cool'd.
A dismal Silence through the Palace went,
And then loud Shreeks the vaulted Marbles rent.   210
Such as the dying Chorus sings by turns,
And to deaf Seas, and ruthless Tempests mourns,
When now they sink, and now the plundring Streams
Break up each Deck, and rip the Oaken seams.
    But thee triumphant hence the firy Carr,   215
And firy Steeds had born out of the Warr,

From the low World, and thankless Men above,
Unto the Kingdom blest of Peace and Love:
We only mourn'd our selves, in thine Ascent,
Whom thou hadst left beneath with Mantle rent.   220
    For all delight of Life thou then didst lose,
When to Command, thou didst thy self Depose;
Resigning up thy Privacy so dear,
To turn the headstrong Peoples Charioteer;
For to be *Cromwell* was a greater thing,   225
Then ought below, or yet above a King:
Therefore thou rather didst thy Self depress,
Yielding to Rule, because it made thee Less.
    For, neither dist thou from the first apply
Thy sober Spirit unto things too High,   230
But in thine own Fields exercisedst long,
An healthful Mind within a Body strong;
Till at the Seventh time thou in the Skyes,
As a small Cloud, like a Mans hand didst rise;
Then did thick Mists and Winds the air deform,   235
And down at last thou pow'rdst the fertile Storm;
Which to the thirsty Land did plenty bring,
But though forewarn'd, o'r-took and wet the King.
    What since he did, an higher Force him push'd
Still from behind, and it before him rush'd,   240
Though undiscern'd among the tumult blind,
Who think those high Decrees by Man design'd.
'Twas Heav'n would not that his Pow'r should cease.
But walk still middle betwixt War and Peace;
Choosing each Stone, and poysing every weight,   245
Trying the Measures of the Bredth and Height;
Here pulling down, and there erecting New,
Founding a firm State by Proportions true.
    When *Gideon* so did from the War retreat,
Yet by the Conquest of two Kings grown great,   250
He on the Peace extends a Warlike power,

And *Is'rel* saw him rase the Tow'r;
And how he *Succouths* Elders durst suppress,
With Thorns and Briars of the Wilderness.
No King might ever such a Force have done; 255
Yet would not he be Lord, nor yet his Son.
　Thou with the same strength, and an Heart as plain,
Didst (like thine Olive) still refuse to Reign;
Though why should others all thy Labor spoil,
And Brambles be anointed with thine Oyl, 260
Whose climbing Flame, without a timely stop,
Had quickly Levell'd every Cedar's top.
Therefore first growing to thy self a Law,
Th' ambitious Shrubs thou in just time didst aw.
　So have I seen at Sea, when whirling Winds, 265
Hurry the Bark, but more the Seamens minds,
Who with mistaken Course salute the Sand,
And threat'ning Rocks misapprehend for Land;
While baleful *Tritons* to the shipwrack guide,
And Corposants along the Tacklings slide. 270
The Passengers all wearyed out before,
Giddy, and wishing for the fatal Shore;
Some lusty Mate, who with more careful Eye
Counted the Hours, and ev'ry Star did spy,
The Helm does from the artless Steersman strain, 275
And doubles back unto the safer Main.
What though a while they grumble discontent,
Saving himself he does their loss prevent.
　'Tis not a Freedome, that where All command;
Nor Tyranny, where One does them withstand: 280
But who of both the Bounders knows to lay
Him as their Father must the State obey.
　Thou, and thine House, like *Noah's* Eight did rest,
Left by the Wars Flood on the Mountains Crest:
And the large Vale lay subject to thy Will, 285
Which thou but as an Husbandman would Till:

And only didst for others plant the Vine
Of Liberty, not drunken with its Wine.
    That sober Liberty which men may have,
That they enjoy, but more they vainly crave: 290
And such as to their Parents Tents do press,
May shew their own, not see his Nakedness.
    Yet such a *Chammish* issue still does rage,
The Shame and Plague both of the Land and Age,
Who watch'd thy halting, and thy Fall deride,   295
Rejoycing when the Foot had slipt aside;
That their new King might be the fifth Scepter shake,
And make the World, by his Example, Quake:
Whose frantique Army should they want for Men
Might muster Heresies, so one were ten.   300
What thy Misfortune, they the Spirit call,
And their Religion only is to Fall.
Oh! *Mahomet!* now couldst thou rise again,
Thy Falling-sickness should have made thee Reign,
While *Feake* and *Simpson* would in many a Tome,   305
Have writ the Comments of thy sacred Foame:
For soon thou mightst have past among their Rant
Wer't but for thine unmoved Tulipant;
As thou must needs have own'd them of thy band
For prophecies fit to be *Alcorand*.   310
    Accursed Locusts, whom your King does spit
Out of the Center of th' unbottom'd Pit;
Wand'rers, Adult'rers, Lyers, *Munser's* rest,
Sorcerers, Atheists, Jesuites, Possest;
You who the Scriptures and the Laws deface   315
With the same liberty as Points and Lace;
Oh Race most hypocritically strict!
Bent to reduce us to the ancient Pict;
Well may you act the *Adam* and the *Eve*;
Ay, and the Serpent too that did deceive.   320
    But the great Captain, now the danger's ore,

Makes you for his sake Tremble one fit more;
And, to your spight, returning yet alive
Does with himself all that is good revive.
So when first Man did through the Morning new   325
See the bright Sun his shining Race pursue,
All day he follow'd with unwearied sight,
Pleas'd with that other World of moving Light;
But thought him when he miss'd his setting beams,
Sunk in the Hills, or plung'd below the Streams.   330
While dismal blacks hung round the Universe,
And Stars (like Tapers) burn'd upon his Herse:
And Owls and Ravens with their screeching noyse
Did make the Fun'rals sadder by their Joyes.
His weeping Eyes the doleful Vigils keep,   335
Not knowing yet the Night was made for sleep:
Still to the West, where he him lost, he turn'd,
And with such accents, as Despairing, mourn'd:
Why did mine Eyes once see so bright a Ray;
Or why Day last no longer then a Day?   340
When streight the Sun behind him he descry'd,
Smiling serenely from the further side.
So while our Star that gives us Light and Heat,
Seem'd now a long and gloomy Night to threat,
Up from the other World his Flame he darts,   345
And Princes shining through their windows starts;
Who their suspected Counsellors refuse,
And credulous Ambassadors accuse.
'Is this, saith one, the Nation that we read
'Spent with both Wars, under a Captain dead?   350
'Yet rig a Navy while we dress us late;
'And ere we Dine, rase and rebuild our State.
'What Oaken Forrests, and what golden Mines!
'What Mints of Men, what Union of Designes!
'Unless their Ships, do, as their Fowle proceed   355
'Of shedding Leaves, that with their Ocean breed.

131

'Theirs are not Ships, but rather Arks of War,
'And beaked Promontories sail'd from far;
'Of floting Islands a new Hatched Nest;
'A Fleet of Worlds, of other Worlds in quest;   360
'An hideous shole of wood-Leviathans,
'Arm'd with three Tire of brazen Hurricans;
'That through the Center shoot their thundring side
'And sink the Earth that does at Anchor ride.
'What refuge to escape them can be found,   365
'Whose watry Leaguers all the world surround?
'Needs must we all their Tributaries be,
'Whose Navies hold the Sluces of the Sea.
'The Ocean is the Fountain of Command,
'But that once took, we Captives are on Land.   370
'And those that have the Waters for their share,
'Can quickly leave us neither Earth nor Air.
'Yet if through these our Fears could find a pass;
'Through double Oak, & lin'd with treble Brass;
'That one Man still, although but nam'd, alarms   375
'More than all Men, all Navies, and all Arms.
'Him, all the Day, Him, in late Nights I dread,
'And still his Sword seems hanging o'er my head.
'The Nation had been ours, but his one Soul
'Moves the great Bulk, and animates the whole.   380
'He Secrecy with Number hath inchas'd,
'Courage with Age, Maturity with Hast:
'The Valiants Terror, Riddle of the Wise;
'And still his Fauchion all our Knots unties.
'Where did he learn those Arts that cost us dear?   385
,Where below Earth, or where above the Sphere?
'He seems a King by long Succession born,
'And yet the same to be a King does scorn.
'Abroad a King he seems, and something more,
'At home a Subject on the equal Floor.   390
'O could I once him with our Title see,

'So should I hope yet he might Dye as wee.
'But let them write his Praise that love him best,
'It grieves me sore to have thus much confest.
  Pardon, great Prince, if thus their Fear or Spight   395
More then our Love and Duty do thee Right.
I yield, nor further will the Prize contend;
So that we both alike may miss our End:
While thou thy venerable Head dost raise
As far above their Malice as my Praise.   400
And as the *Angel* of our Commonweal,
Troubling the Waters, yearly mak'st them Heal.

Two Songs at the Marriage of the Lord Fauconberg and the Lady Mary Cromwell

First

Chorus, Endymion. Luna

Chorus

TH' *Astrologers* own Eyes are set,
And even Wolves the Sheep forget;
Only *this Shepheard*, late and soon,
Upon this Hill outwakes the *Moon*.
Heark how he sings, with sad delight,   5
Thorough the clear and silent Night.

Endymion

Cynthia, O *Cynthia*, turn thine Ear,
Nor scorn *Endymions* plaints to hear.
As we our Flocks, so you command
The fleecy Clouds with silver wand.   10

Cynthia

If thou a *Mortal*, rather sleep;
Or if a *Shepheard*, watch thy Sheep.

Endymion

The *Shepheard*, since he saw thine Eyes,
And *Sheep* are both thy *Sacrifice*.
Nor merits he a *Mortal's* name,   15
That burns with an *immortal Flame*.

Cynthia

I have enough for me to do,
Ruling the Waves that Ebb and flow.

Endymion

Since thou disdain'st not then to share
On Sublunary things they care;   20
Rather restrain these double Seas,
Mine Eyes uncessant deluges.

Cynthia

My wakeful Lamp all night must move,
Securing their Repose above.

Endymion

If therefore thy resplendent Ray   25
Can make a Night more bright then Day;
Shine thorough this obscurer Brest,
With shades of deep Despair opprest.

Chorus

Courage, *Endymion*, boldly Woo,
Anchises was a *Shepheard* too: 30
Yet is *her younger Sister* laid
Sporting with him in *Ida's shade*:

And *Cynthia*, though the strongest
Seeks but the honour to have held out longest.

Endymion

Here unto *Latmos Top* I climbe: 35
How far below thine *Orbe* sublime?
O why, as well as Eyes to see,
Have I not Armes that reach to thee?

Cynthia

'Tis needless then that I refuse,
Would you but your own Reason use.   40

Endymion

Though I so high may not pretend,
It is the same so you descend.

Cynthia

These Stars would say I do them wrong,
Rivals each one for thee too strong.

Endymion

The Stars are fix'd unto their *Sphere*,   45
And cannot, though they would, come near.
Less Loves set of each others praise,
While *Stars* Eclypse by mixing Rayes.

Cynthia

That Cave is dark.

Endymion

                Then none can spy: 50
Or shine Thou there and 'tis the Sky.

Joy to *Endymion*,
For he has *Cynthia's favour won*.
And *Jove* himself approves
With his serenest influence their Loves.   55
For he did never love to pair
His Progeny above the Air;
But to be honest, valiant, wise,
Makes *Mortals* matches fit for *Deityes*.

Second Song

Hobbinol. Phillis. Tomalin

Hobbinol

PHILLIS, *Tomalin*, away:
Never such a merry day.
For *the Northern Shepheards Son*
Has *Menalca's daughter* won.

Phillis

Stay till I some flow'rs ha' ty'd   5
In a Garland for the Bride.

Tomalin

If thou would'st a Garland bring,
Phillis you may wait the Spring:
They ha' chosen such an hour
When *She* is the only flow'r.   10

Phillis

Let's not then at least be seen
Without each a Sprig of Green.

136

Hobbinol

Fear not: at *Menalca's Hall.*
There is Bayes enough for all.
He when Young as we did graze,   15
But when Old he planted Bayes.

Tomalin

Here *She* comes; but with a Look
Far more catching then my Hook.
'Twas those Eyes, I now dare swear,
Led our Lambs we knew not where.   20

Hobbinol

Not our Lambs own Fleeces are
Curl'd so love as her Hair.
Nor our Sheep new Wash'd can be
Half so white or sweet as *She.*

Phillis

He so looks as fit to keep   25
Somewhat else then silly *Sheep.*

Hobbinol

Come, lets in some Carol new
Pay to Love and Them their due.

All

Joy to that *happy Pair,*
Whose Hopes united banish our Despair.   30
  What *Shepheard* could for Love pretend,
Whil'st all the *Nymphs* on *Damon's* choice attend?
  What *Shepherdess* could hope to wed
Before *Marina's* turn were sped?
Now lesser Beauties may take place.   35
And meaner Virtues come in play;

137

While they,
Looking from high,
Shall grace
Our Flocks and us with a propitious Eye.   40
    But what is most, the gentle Swain
    No more shall need of Love complain;
    But Virtue shall be Beauties hire,
And those be equal that have equal Fire.
    Marina yields. Who dares be coy?   45
Or who despair, now *Damon* does enjoy?
        Joy to that happy Pair,
Whose Hopes united banish our Despair.

A Poem upon the Death of O.C.

THAT Providence which had so long the care
Of *Cromwell's* head, and numbred ev'ry hair,
Now in its self (the Glass where all appears)
Had seen the period of his golden Years:
And thenceforth onely did attend to trace,   5
What death might least so fair a Life deface.
    The People, which what most they fear esteem,
Death when more horrid so more noble deem;
And blame the last *Act*, like *Spectators* vain,
Unless the *Prince* whom they applaud be slain.   10
Nor Fate indeed can well refuse that right
To those that liv'd in War, to dye in Fight.
    But long his *Valour* none had left that could
Indanger him, or *Clemency* that would.
And he whom Nature all for Peace had made,   15
But angry Heaven unto War had sway'd,
And so less useful where he most desir'd,

138

For what he least affected was admir'd,
Deserved yet an End whose ev'ry part
Should speak the wondrous softness of his Heart.   20
  To *Love* and *Grief* the fatal Writ was sign'd;
(Those nobler weaknesses of humane Mind,
From which those Powers that issu'd the Decree,
Although immortal, found they were not free.)
That they, to whom his Breast still open lyes,   25
In gentle Passions should his Death disguise:
And leave succeeding Ages cause to mourn,
As long as Grief shall weep, or Love shall burn.
  Streight does a slow and languishing Disease
Eliza, Natures and his darling, seize.   30
Her when an infant, taken with her Charms,
He oft would flourish in his mighty Arms;
And, lest their force the tender burthen wrong,
Slacken the vigour of his Muscles strong;
Then to the Mothers brest her softly move,   35
Which while she drain'd of Milk she filled with Love.
But as with riper Years her Virtue grew,
And ev'ry minute adds a Lustre new;
When with meridian height her Beauty shin'd,
And thorough that sparkled her fairer Mind;   40
When She with Smile serene and Words discreet
His hidden Soul at ev'ry turn could meet;
Then might y' ha' daily his Affection spy'd,
Doubling that knot which Destiny had ty'd.
While they by sence, nor knowing, comprehend   45
How on each other both their Fates depend.
With her each day the pleasing Hours he shares,
And at her Aspect calms his growing Cares;
Or with a Grandsire's joy her Children sees
Hanging about her neck or at his knees.   50
Hold fast dear Infants, hold them both or none;
This will not stay when once the other's gone.

A silent fire now wasts those Limbs of Wax,
And him within his tortur'd Image racks.
So the Flowr with'ring which the Garden crown'd,   55
The sad Root pines in secret under ground.
Each Groan he doubled and each Sigh he sigh'd,
Repeated over to the restless Night.
No trembling String compos'd to Numbers new,
Answers the touch in Notes more sad more true.   60
She lest He grieve hides what She can her pains,
And He to lessen hers his Sorrow feigns:
Yet both perceiv'd, yet both conceal'd their Skills,
And so diminishing increast their ills:
That whether by each others grief they fell,   65
Or on their own redoubled, none can tell.
   And now *Eliza's* purple Locks were shorn,
Where She so long her *Father's* fate had worn:
And frequent lightning to her Soul that flyes,
Devides the Air, and opens all the Skyes: 70
And now his Life, suspended by her breath,
Ran out impetuously to hasting Death.
Like polish'd Mirrours, so his steely Brest
Had ev'ry figure of her woes exprest;
And with the damp of her last Gasps obscur'd,   75
Had drawn such staines as were not to be cur'd.
Fate could not either reach with single stroke,
But the dear Image fled the Mirrour broke.
   Who now shall tell us more of mournful Swans,
Of Halcyons kind, or bleeding Pelicans?   80
No downy breast did ere so gently beat,
Or fan with airy plumes so soft an heat.
For he no duty by his height excus'd,
Nor though a *Prince* to be a *Man* refused:
But rather then in his *Eliza's* pain   85
Not love, not grieve, would neither live nor reign:
And in himself so oft immortal try'd,

Yet in compassion of another dy'd.
   So have I seen a Vine, whose lasting Age
Of many a Winter hath surviv'd the rage.   90
Under whose shady tent Men ev'ry year
At its rich bloods expence their Sorrows chear
If some dear branch where it extends its life
Chance to be prun'd by an untimely knife,
The Parent-Tree unto the Grief succeeds,   95
And through the Wound its vital humour bleeds;
Trickling in watry drops, whose flowing shape
Weeps that it falls ere fix'd into a Grape.
So the dry Stock, no more that spreading Vine,
Frustrates the Autumn and the hopes of Wine.   100
   A secret Cause does sure those Signs ordain
Fore boding Princes falls, and seldom vain.
Whether some Kinder Pow'rs, that wish us well,
What they above cannot prevent, foretell;
Or the great World do by consent presage,   105
As hollow Seas with future Tempests rage:
Or rather Heav'n, which us so long foresees,
Their fun'rals celebrate while it decrees.
But never yet was any humane Fate
By nature solemniz'd with so much state.   110
He unconcern'd the dreadful passage crost;
But oh what pangs that Death did Nature cost!
First the great *Thunder* was shot off, and sent
The Signal from the starry Battlement.
The *Winds* receive it, and its force out-do,   115
As practising how they could thunder too:
Out of the Binders Hand the Shaves they tore,
And thrash'd the Harvest in the airy floore;
Or of huge Trees, whose growth with his did rise,
The deep foundations open'd to the Skyes.   120
Then heavy *Showres* the winged Tempests lead,
And pour the Deluge ore the *Chaos* head.

The Race of warlike *Horses* at his Tomb
Offer themselves in many a *Hecatomb*;
With pensive head towards the ground they fall,   125
And helpless languish at the tainted Stall.
Numbers of *Men* decrease with pains unknown
And hasten not to see his Death their own.
Such Tortures all the Elements unfix'd,
Troubled to part where so exactly mix'd.   130
And as through Air his wasting Spirits flow'd,
The Universe labour'd beneath their load.

    Nature it seem'd with him would Nature vye;
He with *Eliza*, It with him would dye.

    He without noise still travell'd to his End,   135
As silent Suns to meet the Night descend.
The *Stars* that for him fought had only pow'r
Left to determine now his fatal Hour;
Which, since they might not hinder, yet they cast
To chuse it worthy of his *Glories* past.   140

    No part of time but bore his mark away
Of honour; all the Year was *Cromwell's* day:
But this, of all the most auspicious found,
Twice had in open field him Victor crown'd:
When up the armed Mountains of *Dunbar*   145
He march'd, and through deep *Severn* ending war.
What day should him *eternize* but the same
That had before *immortaliz'd* his *Name*?
That so who ere would at his Death have joy'd,
In their own Griefs might find themselves imploy'd;   150
But those that sadly his departure griev'd,
Yet joy'd remembring what he once atchiev'd.
And the last minute his victorious *Ghost*
Gave chase to *Ligney* on the *Belgick Coast*.
Here ended all his mortal toyles: He lay'd   155
And slept in Peace under the *Lawrel shade*.

    O Cromwell, Heavens Favorite! To none

Have such high honours from above been shown:
For whom the Elements we Mourners see,
And *Heav'n* it self would the great *Herald* be;   160
Which with more Care set forth his Obsequies
Then those of *Moses* hid from humane Eyes;
As jealous only here lest all be less,
That we could to his Memory express.

    Then let us to our course of Mourning keep: 165
Where *Heaven* leads, 'tis Piety to weep.
Stand back ye Seas, and shrunk beneath the vail
Of your Abysse, with cover'd Head bewail
Your *Monarch*: We demand not your supplies
To compass in our *Isle*; our Tears suffice: 170
Since him away the dismal Tempest rent,
Who once more joyn'd us to the Continent;
Who planted *England* on the *Flandrick shoar*,
And stretched *our frontire* to the *Indian Ore*;
Whose greater *Truths* obscure the *Fables* old,   175
Whether of *Brittish Saints or Worthy's* told;
And in a valour less'ning *Arthur's* deeds,
For Holyness the *Confessor* exceeds.

    He first put Armes into *Religions* hand,
And tim'rous *Conscience* unto *Courage* man'd: 180
The Souldier taught that inward Mail to wear,
And *fearing God* how they should *nothing fear*.
Those Strokes he said will pierce through all below
Where those that strike from Heaven fetch their Blow.
Astonish'd armyes did their flight prepare,   185
And Cityes strong were stormed by his prayer;
Of that for ever *Preston's* field shall tell
The story, and impregnable *Clonmell*.
And where the sandy mountain *Fenwick* scal'd,
The sea between, yet hence his pray'r prevail'd.   190
What man was ever so in Heavn't obey'd
Since the commanded sun o're *Gibeon* stay'd?

In all his warrs needs must he triumph, when
He conquer'd *God*, still ere he fought with men:
Hence, though in battle none so brave or fierce,   195
Yet him the adverse steel could never pierce.
Pity it seem'd to hurt him more that felt
Each wound himself which he to others delt;
Danger itself refusing to offend
So loose an enemy, so fast a friend.   200
   Friendship, that sacred virtue, long dos claime
The first foundation of his house and name:
But within one its narrow limits fall,
His tendernesse extended unto all.
And that deep soule through every channell flows,   205
Where kindly nature loves itself to lose.
More strong affections never reason serv'd,
Yet still affected most what best deserv'd.
If he *Eliza* lov'd to that degree,
(Though who more worthy to be lov'd than she?)   210
If so indulgent to his own, how deare
To him the children of the Highest were?
For her he once did nature's tribute pay:
For these his life adventur'd every day:
And 'twould be found, could we his thoughts have cast,   215
Their griefs struck deepest, if *Eliza's* last.
   What prudence more than humane did he need
To keep so deare, so diff'ring mindes agreed?
The worser sort, so conscious of their ill,
Lye weak and easy to the ruler's will;   220
But to the good (too many or too few)
All law is useless, all reward is due.
Oh ill advis'd, if not for love, for shame,
Spare yet your own, if you neglect his fame;
Least others dare to think your zeale a maske,   225
And you to govern only Heaven's taske.
   Valour, religion, friendship, prudence dy'd

At once with him, and all that's good beside;
And we death's refuse Nature's dregs confin'd
To loathsome life, Alas! are left behind   230
Where we (so once we us'd) shall now no more,
To fetch day, presse about his chamber-door;
From which he issu'd with that awfull state,
It seem'd Mars broke through *Janus'* double gate;
Yet always temper'd with an Aire so mild,   235
No *April* sunns that ere so gently smil'd;
No more shall heare that powerful language charm,
Whose force oft spar'd the labour of his arm:
No more shall follow where he spent the dayes
In warre, in counsell, or in pray'r, and praise;   240
Whose meanest acts he would himself advance,
As ungirt *David* to the arke did dance.
All, all is gone of ours or his delight
In horses fierce, wild deer, or armour bright;
Francisca faire can nothing now but weep,   245
Nor with soft notes shall sing his cares asleep.
    I saw him dead, a leaden slumber lyes,
And mortal sleep over those wakefull eyes:
Those gentle Rays under the lids were fled,
Which through his looks that piercing sweetnesse shed;   250
That port which so Majestique was and strong,
Loose and depriv'd of vigour, stretch'd along:
All wither'd, all discolour'd, pale and wan,
How much another thing, no more that man?
Oh humaine glory, vaine, Oh death, oh wings,   255
Oh worthlesse world oh transitory things!
Yet dwelt that greatnesse in his shape decay'd
That still though dead, greater than death he lay'd;
And in his alter'd face you something faigne,
That threatens death, he yet will live againe.   260
    Not much unlike the sacred Oak, which shoots
To Heav'n its branches, and through earth its roots:

Whose spacious boughs are hung with Trophies round,
And honour'd wreaths have oft the victour crown'd.
When angry *Jove* darts lightning through the Aire,   265
At mortalls sins, nor his own plant will spare;
(It groans, and bruises all below that stood
So many yeares the shelter of the wood.)
The tree ere while foreshortned to our view,
When fall'n shews taller yet than as it grew: 270
   So shall his praise to after times increase,
When truth shall be allow'd, and faction cease;
And his own shadows with him fall; the eye
Detracts from objects than itself more high:
But when death takes them from that envy'd Seate,   275
Seeing how little we confess, how greate;
Thee, many ages hence, in martial verse
Shall th' *English* souldier, ere he charge, rehearse;
Singing of thee, inflame themselves to fight,
And with the name of *Cromwell*, armyes fright.   280
As long as rivers to the seas shall runne,
As long as *Cynthia* shall relieve the sunne,
While staggs shall fly unto the forests thick,
While sheep delight the grassy downs to pick,
As long as future time succeeds the past,   285
Always thy honour, praise and name, shall last.
   Thou in a pitch how farre beyond the sphere
Of humane glory towr'st, and raigning there
Despoyl'd of mortall robes, in seas of blisse,
Plunging dost bathe and tread the bright abysse: 290
There thy great soule at once a world does see,
Spacious enough, and pure enough for thee.
How soon thou *Moses* hast, and *Joshua* found,
And *David*, for the sword and harpe renown'd?
How streight canst to each happy mansion goe?   295
(Farr better known above than here below:)
And in those joyes dost spend the endlesse day,

146

Which in expressing, we ourselves betray.

For we, since thou art gone, with heavy doome,
Wander like ghosts about thy loved tombe;   300
And lost in tears, have neither sight nor minde
To guide us upward through this Region blinde.
Since thou art gone, who best that way could'st teach,
Onely our sighs, perhaps, may thither reach.

And *Richard* yet, where his great Parent led,   305
Beats on the rugged track: He, vertue dead,
Revives; and by his milder beams assures;
And yet how much of them his griefe obscures.

He, as his father, long was kept from sight
In private, to be view'd by better light;   310
But open'd once, what splendour dos he throw?
A *Cromwell* in an houre a prince will grow.
How he becomes that seat, how strongly streins,
How gently winds at once the ruling Reins?
Heav'n to this choice prepar'd a Diadem,   315
Richer then any Eastern silk, or gemme;
A pearly rainbow, where the Sun inchas'd
His brows, like an Imperiall Jewel grac'd.

We find already what those Omens mean,
Earth nere more glad, nor Heaven more serene.   320
Cease now our griefs, calme peace succeeds a war,
Rainbow to storms, *Richard* to *Oliver*.
Tempt not his clemency to try his pow'r,
He threats no Deluge, yet foretells a showre.

OTHER ENGLISH POEMS
AND SELECTED SATIRES

To his Noble Friend Mr. Richard Lovelace, upon his Poems

Sir,

    Our times are much degenerate from those
Which your sweet Muse which your fair Fortune chose,
And as complexions alter with the Climes,
Our wits have drawne th' infection of our times.
That candid Age no other way could tell   5
To be ingenious, but by speaking well.
Who best could prayse, had then the greatest prayse,
Twas more esteemed to give, then weare the Bayes:
Modest ambition studi'd only then,
To honour not her selfe, but worthy men.   10
These vertues now are banisht out of Towne,
Our Civill Wars have lost the Civicke crowne.
He highest builds, who with most Art destroys,
And against others Fame his owne employs.
I see the envious Caterpillar sit   15
On the faire blossome of each growing wit.
    The Ayre's already tainted with the swarms
Of Insects which against you rise in arms.
Word-peckers, Paper-rats, Book-scorpions,
Of wit corrupted, the unfashion'd Sons.   20
The barbed Censurers begin to looke
Like the grim consistory on thy Booke;
And on each line cast a reforming eye,
Severer then the young Presbytery.
Till when in vaine they have thee all perus'd,   25
You shall for being faultlesse be accus'd.
You wrong'd in her the Houses Priviledge.

Some that you under sequestration are,
Because you write when going to the Warre,   30
And one the Book prohibits, because *Kent*
Their first Petition by the Authour sent.
    But when the beauteous Ladies came to know
That their deare *Lovelace* was endanger'd so:
Lovelace that thaw'd the most congealed brest,   35
He who lov'd best and them defended best.
Whose hand so rudely grasps the steely brand,
Whose hand so gently melts the Ladies hand.
They all in mutiny though yet undrest
Sally'd and would in his defence contest.   40
And one the loveliest that was yet e're seen,
Thinking that I too of the rout had been,
Mine eyes invaded with a female spight
(She knew what pain 'twould be to lose that sight.)
O no, mistake not, I reply'd, for I   45
In your defence, or in his cause would dy.
But he secure of glory and of time
Above their envy, or mind aid doth clime.
Him, valianst men, and fairest Nymphys approve,
His Booke in them finds Judgement, with you Love.   50

Upon the Death of Lord Hastings

Go, intercept some Fountain in the Vein,
Whose Virgin-Source yet never steept the Plain
Hastings is dead, and we must finde a Store
Of Tears untoucht, and never wept before.
Go, stand betwixt the *Morning* and the *Flowers*;   5
And, ere they fall, arrest the early *Showers*.

Hastings is dead; and we, disconsolate,
With early *Tears* must morn his early *Fate*.
   Alas, his *Vertues* did his *Death* presage:
Needs must he die, that doth out-run his *Age*.   10
The Phlegmatick and Slowe prolongs his day,
And on Times Wheel sticks like a *Remora*.
What man is he, that hath not *Heaven* beguil'd,
And is not thence mistaken for a *Childe*?
While those of growth more sudden, and more bold,   15
Are hurried hence, as if already old.
For, there above, They number not as here,
But weigh to Man the *Geometrick* yeer.
   Had he but at this Measure still increast,
And on *the Tree of Life* once made a Feast,   20
As that of *Knowledge*; what Loves had he given
To Earth, and then what Jealousies to Heaven!
But 't is a *Maxime* of that State, That none,
Lest He become like Them, taste more than one.
Therefore the *Democratick* Stars did rise,   25
And all that Worth from hence did *Ostracize*.
   Yet as some *Prince*, that, for State-Jealousie,
Secures his neerest and most lov'd *Ally*;
His Thought with richest Triumphs entertains,
And in the choicest Pleasures charms his Pains: 30
So he, not banisht hence, but there confin'd,
There better recreates his active Minde.
   Before the *Chrystal Palace* where he dwells
The armed *Angels* hold their Carouzels;
And underneath, he views the *Turnaments*   35
Of all these Sublunary *Elements*.
But most he doth th' *Eternal Book* behold,
On which the *happie Names* do stand enroll'd;
And gladly there can all his Kindred claim
But most rejoyces at his *Mothers* name.   40
   The gods themselves cannot their Joy conceal,

153

But draw their Viels, and their pure Beams reveal:
Onely they drooping *Hymeneus* note,
Who for sad *Purple* tears his *Saffron*-coat;
And trails his Torches th'row the Starry Hall   45
Reversed, at his *Darlings* Funeral.

    And *Æsculapius*, who, asham'd and stern,
Himself at once condemneth, and *Mayern*;
Like some sad *Chymist*, who, prepar'd to reap
The *Golden Harvest*, sees his Glasses leap.   50
For, how Immortal must their race have stood,
Had *Mayern* once been mixt with *Hastings* blood!
How Sweet and Verdant would these *Lawrels* be,
Had they been planted on that *Balsam*-tree!

    But what could he, good man, although he bruis'd   55
All Herbs, and them a thousand ways infus'd?
All he had try'd, but all in vain, he saw,
And wept, as we, without Redress or Law.
For *Man* (alas) is but the *Heavens* sport;
And *Art* indeed is Long, but *Life* is Short.   60

An Elegy upon the Death of my Lord Francis Villiers

TIS true that he is dead: but yet to chuse,
Methinkes thou Fame should not have brought the news
Thou canst discourse at will and speak at large:
But wast not in the fight nor durst thou charge.
While he transported all with valient rage   5
His Name eternizd, but cut short his age;
On the safe battlements of Richmonds bowers
Thou was espyd, and from the guilded Towers

Thy silver Trumpets sounded a Retreat,
Farre from the dust and battails sulphry heat. 10
Yet what couldst thou have done? 'tis alwayes late
To struggle with inevitable fate.
Much rather thou I know expectst to tell
How heavy *Cromwell* gnasht the earth and fell.
Or how slow Death farre from the sight of day 15
The long-deceived *Fairfax* bore away.
But untill then, let us young *Francis* praise:
And plant upon his hearse the bloody bayes,
Which we will water with our welling eyes.
Teares spring not still from spungy Cowardice. 20
The purer fountains from the Rocks more steep
Destill and stony valour best doth weep.
Besides Revenge, if often quencht in teares,
Hardens like Steele and daily keener weares.

   Great *Buckingham* whose death doth freshy strike 25
Our memoryes, because to this so like;
Ere that in the Eternal Court he shone,
And here a Favorite there found a throne;
The fatall night before he hence did bleed,
Left to his *Princess* this immortal seed. 30
As the wise *Chinese* in the fertile wombe
Of Earth doth a more precious clay entombe,
Which dying by his will he leaves consigned:
Till by mature delay of time refind
The christall metall fit to the release 35
Is taken forth to crowne each royal feast:
Such was the fate by which this Postume breathed
Who scarcely seems begotten but bequeathd.

   Never was any humane plant that grew
More faire then this and acceptably new. 40
'Tis truth that beauty doth most men dispraise:
Prudence and valour their esteeme do raise.
But he that hath already these in store,

Can not be poorer sure for having more.
And his unimitable handsomenesse   45
Made him indeed be more then man, not less.
We do but faintly gods resemblance beare
And like rough coyns of carelesse mints appeare:
But he of purpose made, did represent
In a rich Medall every lineament.   50
   Lovely and admirable as he was,
Yet was his Sword or Armour all his Glasse.
Nor in his Mistris eyes that joy he tooke,
As in an Enemies himselfe to looke.
I know how well he did, with what delight   55
Those serious imitations of fight.
Still in the trialls of strong exercise
His was the first, and his the second prize.
   Bright Lady, thou that rulest from above
The last and greatest Monarchy of Love: 60
Faire *Richmond* hold thy Brother or he goes.
Try if the Jasmin of thy hand or Rose
Of thy red Lip can keep him always here.
For he lives danger and doth never feare.
Or may thy tears prevaile with him to stay?   65
   But he resolv'd breaks carelessly away.
Onely one argument could now prolong
His stay and that most faire and so most strong:
The matchless *Chlora* whose pure fires did warm
His soule and only could his passions charme.   70
   You might with much more reason go reprove
The amorous Magnet which the North doth love.
Or preach divorce and say it is amisse
That with tall Elms the twining Vines should kisse
Then chide two such so fit, so equall faire   75
That in the world they have no other paire.
Whom it might seeme that Heaven did create
To restore man unto his first estate.

Yet she for honours tyrannous respect
Her own desires did and his neglect.   80
And like the Modest Plant at every touch
Shrunk in her leaves and feard it was too much.
   But who can paint the torments and that pain
Which he profest and now she could not faigne?
He like the Sun but overcast and pale: 85
Shee like a Rainbow, that ere long must faile,
Whose rosiall cheek where Heaven it selfe did view
Begins to separate and dissolve to dew.
   At last he leave obtaines though sad and slow,
First of her and then of himselfe to goe.   90
How comely and how terrible he sits
At once and Warre as well as Love befits!
Ride where thou wilt and bold adventures find:
But all the Ladies are got up behind.
Guard them, though not thy selfe: for in thy death   95
Th' Eleven thousand Virgins lost their breath.
   So *Hector* issuing from the Trojan wall
The sad *Iliades* to the Gods did call
With hands displayed and with dishevell' haire
That they the Empire in his life would spare.   100
While he secure through all the field doth spy
Achilles for *Achilles* only cry.
Ah ignorant that yet e're night he must
Be drawn by him inglorious through the dust.
   Such fell young *Villiers* in the chearfull heat   105
Of youth: his locks intangled all with sweat
And those eyes which the Sentinell did keep
Of love closed up in an eternall sleep.
While *Venus* of *Adonis* thinks no more
Slaine by the harsh tuske of the Savage Boare.   110
Hither she runns and hath him hurried farre
Out of the noise and blood, and killing warre:
Where in her Gardens of Sweet myrtle laid,

She kisses him in the immortall shade,
    Yet dyed he not revengelesse: Much he did   115
Ere he could suffer. A whole Pyramid
Of Vulgar bodies he erected high:
Scorning without a Sepulcher to dye.
And with his steele which did whole troops divide
He cuts his Epitaph on either Side.   120
Till finding nothing to his courage fit
He rid up last to death and conquer'd it.
    Such are the Obsequies to *Francis* own:
He best the pompe of his owne death have showne.
And we hereafter to his honour will   125
Not write so many, but so many kill.
Till the whole Army by just vengeance come
To be at once his Trophee and his Tombe.

From *The Loyal Scot*

NOT so brave Douglass, on whose Lovely Chin   15
The Early down but newly did begin,
And modest beauty yet his sex did vail,
Whilst Envious virgins hope hee is a Male.
His shady locks Curl back themselves to seek
Nor other Courtship knew but to his Cheek.   20
Oft as hee in Chill Eske or Seyne by night
Hardned and Cool'd those Limbs soe soft, soe white,
Among the Reeds to bee espy'd by him
The Nymphs would Rustle, hee would forward swim:
They sigh'd and said 'fond boy why soe Untame,   25
That flyst loves fires reserv'd for other flame?'
Fix'd on his ship hee fac'd the horrid day
And wonder'd much at those that Runne away,

Nor other fear himself cold Comprehend
Then least Heaven fall ere thither hee Ascend.   30
With birding at the Dutch, as though in sport,
Hee entertains the while his life too short,
Or waves his sword and, Cou'd hee them Conjure,
Within its Circle knows himself secure.
The fatall bark him boards with Grapling fire   35
And safely through its ports the Dutch retire.
That pretious life hee yet disdaines to save
Or with known art to try the Gentle Wave.
Much him the glories of his Antient Race
Inspire, nor cold hee his own Deeds deface;   40
And secrett Joy in his own soul doth Rise
That Monk lookes on to see how Douglass dies.
Like a glad lover the fierce Flames hee meets,
And tries his first Imbraces in their sheets.
His shape Exact which the bright flames enfold   45
Like the sun's Statue stands of burnisht Gold:
Round the Transparent fire about him Glowes
As the Clear Amber on the bee doth Close;
And as on Angells head their Glories shine
His burning Locks Adorn his face divine.   50
But when in his Imortall mind hee felt
His Altred form and sodred Limbs to Melt,
Down on the Deck hee laid him down and dy'd
With his dear sword reposing by his side,
And on his flaming Planks soe rests his head   55
As one that Huggs himself in a Warm bed.
The ship burnes down and with his reliques sinks,
And the sad stream beneath his Ashes drinks.
Fortunate Boy, if ere my verse may Claim
That Matchless grace to propagate thy fame,   60
When Oeta and Alcides are forgott,
Our English youth shall sing the valiant Scott.
Skip Sadles: Pegasus thou needst not Bragg,

Sometimes the Gall'way Proves the better Nagg.
Shall not a death soe Generous now when told   65
Unite our distance, fill the breaches old?
Such in the Roman forum Curtius brave
Galloping down Clos'd up the Gaping Cave.
Noe more discourse of Scotch or English Race
Nor Chaunt the fabulous hunt of Chivy Chase: 70
Mixt in Corinthian Mettall at thy Flame
Our nations Melting thy Colossus Frame,
Shall fix a foot on either neighbouring Shore
And Joyn those Lands that seemed to part before.

From *The Loyal Scot*

When daring Blood to have his rents regain'd
Upon the English Diadem distrain'd,
Hee Chose the Cassock Circingle and Gown,   180
The fittest Mask for one that Robs a Crown.
But his Lay pitty underneath prevailed
And while hee spared the keepers life hee fail'd.
With the preists vestments had hee but put on
A Bishops Cruelty, the Crown had gone.   185

COMMENTARY

14. **TO THE READER**
'Mary Marvell' was not Marvell's wife. See introduction, pp. 3–4.

15. **A DIALOGUE, BETWEEN THE RESOLVED SOUL, AND CREATED PLEASURE**

This poem, while not one of Marvell's best (but F. W. Bradbrook includes it in a group of poems in which Marvell's 'quality is best seen'), has some distinction as an exercise in the tradition of the poetic dialogue between soul and body, or spirit and flesh, which goes back to the Middle Ages. Although playful, it shows Marvell's concern with a theme very much in the air during the age of Puritan emergence. It seems likely that its form was conditioned by its having been intended for music, though no musical setting has been discovered. Note that the contrast between the speeches of Pleasure and the Soul is reflected in a metrical difference: those of the former are in trochaic heptasyllabics, the latter in iambic octobsyllabics. 'There is a suggestion of the dance as well as of the debate.'

l.3. i.e. Shut down your visor as for battle.

l.18. *bait:* take refreshment.

l.21. *plain:* flat, level.

l.22 *Leaf:* petal; *strain:* hurt.

ll.3–12. *vie which:* compete as to which.

l.36. *but:* only.

ll.37–40. It is the music that calls back the hurrying winds and suspends the rivers' flow.

l.43. *chain:* (i) fetter, (ii) alludes to the chains on board ship to fasten shrouds.

l.44. *Chordage:* (1) chords in music, (2) bonds.

ll.46–7. *fence The Batteries:* ward off the assaults.

l.51. *Soft:* M cos F.

l.71. i.e. Find out how deep the centre of the earth is.

ll.73–4. It is not the degree of knowledge by which a man reaches heaven, but the degree of humility.

19. **ON A DROP OF DEW**

Marvell attempted this theme in a Latin poem, *Ros*, as well as in English. The Latin is not printed here, but it is sometimes useful as a guide to the sense and intentions of the English, just as the Latin *Hortus* is to *The Garden*. It resembles one of Vaughan's poems, *The Water-fall*, but as this was not published until 1656, it seems unlikely that Marvell could have seen it before he wrote *On a Drop of Dew*. Could Vaughan, however, have seen a copy of Marvell's poem in MS.? The construction of *On a Drop of Dew*, a highly concentrated exercise in comparisons, is simple: the first 18 lines compare a drop of dew to the soul, the next 18 reverse the process by comparing the soul to a drop of dew. Then follows a four-line conclusion. This is, again, a somewhat cold and formal poem by the standards of Marvell's finest, but it is done with skill, beauty and elegance.

l.3. *blowing:* flowering.

l.4. *Yet:* i.e. as yet.

l.5. *For:* on account of *clear Region*, i.e. heaven.

l.8. *native Element:* i.e. heaven.

ll.9–10. The dew appears to disdain its new home, the purple flower, whose surface it scarcely touches.

ll.13–15. i.e. it weeps because it has been separated from heaven, its true home.

l.23. *green:* fresh.

l.24. *recollecting:* collecting again.

l.27. *coy:* shy, retiring.

l.29. 'Thus shutting out the world on every side' (M).

ll.35–6. Being a sphere, theoretically the dewdrop touches only at its lowest point: the rest aspires to heaven.

l.37. *Manna:* the food of the Israelites in the wilderness, see Exodus XII.

20. THE CORONET

This is what L calls a 'serious religious pastoral poem'. The theme of lust is only very delicately implied—in the poet's resolution to crown Christ's head with the flowers (i.e. poems) with which he previously crowned his mistress. The basic meaning is that the poet ambitiously attempts to redress the wrong that his sins have done Christ by crowning Him, not with thorns, but with his best works, hopes and thoughts. There is a characteristically ironic note in the parenthesis, 'my fruits are only flow'rs': Marvell is saying, 'everything I do is fruitless anyway', which hints that this is one of his false motives for thus attempting to dedicate himself to Christ. And indeed, he does find that the serpent—with all its implications—lies entwined in his garland. To be truthful, therefore, all the poet can do is to ask Christ to grant that his garland may be trampled upon, thus gaining the distinction of crowning his feet.

ll.1–4. Syntactically obscure. The meaning must be: 'When, in place of the thorns with which for a long time—too long—I have crowned my Saviour's head, causing Him many a piercing wound, I seek to redress that wrong by crowning Him with garlands.'

l.7.   Towers: tall head-dress for a woman.

l.14.   twining in: entwining; *speckled breast:* borrowed from Spenser. The point is that the serpent looks like the flowers.

l.22.   curious frame: refers to the elaborate wreath he has made.

ll.23–4. The meaning is: 'and let these flowers, though set with skill . . . wither, so that the serpent may die'.

21. EYES AND TEARS

The material of *Eyes and Tears*, the superiority of sorrow over joy, weeping over laughter, and the theme of Magdalene washing Christ's feet with her tears, was commonplace in 17th-century minor verse. Marvell treats it with a wit reminiscent of Donne, but with his own ironic urbanity. Although it is 'metaphysical', its grave, almost humorous sweetness is entirely personal.

l.3.   object vain: objective reality, in the tradition in which this poem is written, is always regarded as 'vanity' and spiritually unprofitable.

ll.5–8. Sorrow (tears) is a truer measure of reality than mere physical sight.

ll.17–20. In all the gardens the only honey was that to be extracted by sorrow.

l.35.   Cynthia teeming: the waxing moon.

l.38.   it: its. This is a very late use of 'it' for the possessive.

ll.41–2. What is precious to heaven is not the perfume of incense but the fact that it is derived from aromatic gums 'wept' from trees.

23. BERMUDAS

In 1653 Marvell was living at Eton as tutor to Cromwell's ward, William Dutton, in the home of the Puritan divine, John Oxenbridge. Oxenbridge had made two voyages to the Bermudas, in 1634/5, after Archbishop Laud (the 'Prelat' of line 12) had deprived him of his Oxford tutorship. The Bermudas would have suggested to readers of the poem a haven for Puritans from the persecutions of Laud. It is to be noted that this is a very unaustere, even gay, kind of Puritanism. Doubtless the poem was written for Oxenbridge.

l.9.   wracks: wrecks, i.e. casts up on shore.

l.20.   Ormus: Hormuz, on the Persian gulf.

l.23.   Apples: pineapples.

l.28.   Proclaime: make known; *Ambergris:* a fragrant excretion of the sperm whale.

25. CLORINDA AND DAMON

A dialogue in the manner of the Spenserian pastoral between the claims of the flesh and those of the spirit. Some of Marvell's critics assume this to be a piece of Puritan propaganda—and so ostensibly it may have been—yet there is no internal evidence for such a view: Marvell's personal position is ambiguous. The poem is a shade lighthearted, in any case, for Puritan propaganda. Pan was a pagan god, which might have amused Marvell while deceiving his reader, used to a convention.

ll.3-4. A heraldic description of a flowery meadow.

l.8. *vade:* disappear (Latin *vadere*, to pass away).

l.19. *And . . . change?:* Why the sudden change?

ll.21-3. 'My interests have turned from love to religious poetry.'

l.25. He is suggesting that she should be converted to his way of thinking.

26. A DIALOGUE BETWEEN THE SOUL AND BODY

The theme of this brilliant poem was commonplace during the Middle Ages; then it disappeared, to be revived, by Vaughan and others, early in the 17th century. It is difficult to agree with L when he says that the poem is incomplete 'and seems rather to stop than to conclude', although its irregularity might seem to suggest that Marvell deleted some lines. A point worth debating is whether it is, strictly speaking, a religious poem: does not Marvell delight in sheer intellectual high spirits rather than in taking sides in the dialogue? To a poet of his calibre, 'taking sides' would represent a certain vulgarity. Nevertheless, the poem has a grave and original beauty and a satisfying poetic balance. Marvell never shows himself more, in Keats's phrase, 'the chameleon poet', as distinct from the philosopher or the preacher. The compactness of the poem largely depends, as L says, on its consisting of metaphors rather than similes.

l.3. *that . . . stands:* The antecedent of the relative pronoun 'that' is 'Soul'.

ll.5-6. Compare Hopkins' early poem, *The Habit of Perfection*.

l.10. *double:* false, deceitful.

ll.13-14. It is by virtue of possessing a soul that man is upright, unlike the four-footed beasts. 'Impales' may well suggest 'crucifies'. (It is a terrible responsibility to have a soul, and therefore inhibiting to the body's pleasures.)

l.17. The soul needs a place wherein to exercise its spite.

ll.23-4. The soul is exempt from physical feeling and yet, paradoxically, is aware of the pain of confinement in the body.

27. THE NYMPH COMPLAINING FOR THE DEATH OF HER FAUN

Some critics take this poem at its face value, i.e. as a sustained lament by a young girl for a pet wantonly slaughtered by foraging Roundheads. They have instanced earlier laments, such as those by Catullus and Skelton. It seems unlike Marvell, however, to compose a long poem of this sort without hidden undertones: he could not help being subtle. It is evident that the infant faun represents (among other things) the virginity which her lover, Sylvio, disappointed her by not taking; but the virginity which she did not lose at his hands has been taken by, or perhaps even given to, the 'wanton troopers'. She concludes the lament by vowing herself to chastity. Therefore the poem is, essentially, a lament for a certain kind of innocence.

l.11.   Joyn: add: 'I will weep as well as pray'.

ll.16–17.   Deodands are personal chattels which, because they have caused a person's death, are forfeit to the Crown. Thus men, by slaying even beasts unjustly, become deodands forfeit to God.

l.34.   This: i.e. the faun; *grew wild:* (Sylvio) went elsewhere for erotic pleasure.

l.53.   then: than, as in *l.*61.

l.70.   four: This is pronounced as a disyllable, 'fower'.

l.71.   Garden: This is the garden of virgin love, from medieval allegory, and from *The Song of Songs.* Roses and lilies in conjunction are symbols of chaste passion.

l.99.   Heliades: The Heliades were sisters of Phaeton who, on the death of their brother, were metamorphosed into poplar trees (some authorities say willows, which weep) on the banks of a great river.

31.   YOUNG LOVE

l.1.   Infant: Marvell here means not a baby but a girl not yet nubile.

l.6.   beguil'd: entertained and at the same time deceived.

l.9.   stay: wait for.

l.11.   green: immature.

l.21.   'In this way we score a victory over uncertain fate.'

33.   TO HIS COY MISTRESS

Justly regarded as one of Marvell's finest and most delicately balanced poems, this is a characteristically original variation on the Horatian theme of *Carpe diem*—'Gather ye rosebuds while ye may'. Marvell perfectly sustains a subtle tension between witty, ironic lightness and deep seriousness. To regard either tone as predominant is to misunderstand the poem.

l.2.   coyness: sexual unwillingness.

l.10.   Conversion of the Jews: i.e. for ever.

l.11.   vegetable: vegetative; capable of growth and self-propagation, like plant-life.

l.19.   State: solemn progress.

l.24.   'Eternity' was pronounced 'etarnity', thus emphasizing the open vowels, suggesting wide spaces, in 'desarts' (stressed on second syllable) and 'vast'.

l.29.   dust: Cooke + durst F.

l.34.   glew: This is the F reading, as distinct from the usual emendation, 'dew'. M reads 'lew' ('warmth'). We see no strong reason to abandon F, which in its sense of 'glow' seems to us appropriate. Grierson thought that 'glew' was intended in the sense of 'cherry-tree glue'; the original meaning of the noun was 'bird-lime'.

*ll.*39–40. 'Let us rather consume Time, the slow-devouring beast, than be consumed by him.' 'At once' points the contrast between the speed of the consumption of time which is advocated and the slowness of the alternative.

*ll.*43–4. The metaphor is partly sexual; what Marvell is arguing here contrasts sharply with Damon's attitude in *Clorinda and Damon*.

34. THE UNFORTUNATE LOVER

Many of the allusions in this strange poem are obscure. Its theme is a description of the various situations in which the lover finds himself from birth to death, in 'a succession of huge and extravagant metaphors, emblems, or allegories' (L). The sheer ingenuity of the poem, which was probably written for an exclusive literary group, robs it of some of its feeling; at the same time it would be wrong to deny the basic sincerity of the underlying conception of love as a perpetual torment. The title does not refer to a particular unfortunate lover, but implies that to be a lover is to be unfortunate. At her birth, Venus, Goddess of Love, rose from the sea.

*l.*36. *bill:* peck.

*l.*40. *Amphibium:* A singular form of amphibia, beings equally at home on land or in water; here also a being with the seeds of both life and death in it.

*l.*44. *at sharp:* with sharpened weapons, i.e. 'unbaited foils', without guards.

*l.*46. *wing'd Artillery:* the arrows of Cupid.

*l.*48. On his return from Troy Ajax battled with the elements, but was eventually drowned.

*ll.*55–6. The Verb 'relish' is used intransitively in this sentence.

*l.*57. *Banneret:* A knight dubbed on the field of battle.

*l.*64. The metaphor here is heraldic: the lover is seen as scarlet in a black field.

37. THE GALLERY

This is a somewhat more personalised variation on the theme of *The Unfortunate Lover:* of love as a misfortune. Here the lover is tormented by the different aspects of his mistress, who appears in his mental picture-gallery both as the delightful and innocent girl with whom he first fell in love and the relentless, perhaps corrupted demoness. If 'were' in line 48 refers to the past, which it seems to do, then this cannot have been written before July 1650, when Charles I's pictures at Whitehall were dispersed and sold by Act of Parliament.

*l.*5. *Arras:* famous for its tapestries.

*l.*11. *Examining:* testing.

*l.*35.   *Halcyons:* kingfishers.
*l.*40.   *Smell:* i.e. sense of smell.

40. MOURNING

MCB & GL-T's account of this highly intellectual and ironic poem can hardly be bettered. They point out that 'there is a single flash of illumination which holds the poem together'. Marvell is satirizing the superficialities of the tradition of courtly love; and 'at that point where the satirical intention reveals itself, there is a clear direct metaphor of natural beauty, which recalls to the mind something more satisfying and more lovely than is known in this world of polite society'.

*ll.*1–2.   Marvell is ironically addressing those who claim to be able to interpret human motives from the stars.

*ll.*3–4.   The next four stanzas make it clear that the puzzle is whether Chlora is genuinely weeping for a lost lover (Strephon) or merely affecting sorrow while she awaits a new lover.

*l.*13.   *pretending Art:* the 'some affirm' that Chlora pretends art.

*l.*20.   Danäe, mother of Perseus, was impregnated by Zeus in the guise of a shower of gold. The implication of Marvell's witty conceit, put into the mouth of the more cynical bystanders, is that Chlora was narcissistically wooing herself.

*l.*27.   *Donatives:* gifts, i.e. tears.

*ll.*29–36.   The picture of the pearl-fisher is 'the image of natural beauty' referred to above. The real truth of the situation, according to Marvell, is profounder than anything dreamed of by the bystanders (the 'some' of line 13, and the 'bolder' of line 21). Women are more enigmatic than any superficial judgement can ever allow: Marvell for his part is prepared to believe that when a woman weeps she is partially sincere.

41. DAPHNIS AND CHLOE

This poem has a similar structure to the last. First there is an evocation of the artificial pastoral convention, then an image of natural beauty (XXII) as a transition to the realistic conclusion. By being too coy towards her lover and relenting too late, Chloe causes Daphnis to suffer a revulsion against idealistic love, ending in a disillusioned promiscuity.

*ll.*9–12.   As soon as Chloe realized that she was going to lose Daphnis, she was prepared to yield everything.

*ll.*13–16.   'Nature itself, too, is in the habit of discarding its normal order in case the world should disintegrate: a violent disruption may unite more closely.' A typical Metaphysical paradox, incorporating current scientific notions.

167

*l.*15.   *separate:* 'withdraw from conjugal cohabitation' (NED).

*l.*61.   'Absence by itself is enough punishment.'

*l.*78.   *the Gourmand Hebrew:* See *Numbers* Ch. IX.

*ll.*79–80.   F reads 'While he Quailes and Manna fed,/And does through the Desert err'. This does not make sense, and Cooke's sensible emendation in his 1726 edition (reissued 1772), given here, has become standard.

*ll.*81–4.   It was widely believed that those who gathered ferns on Midsummer Eve could attain invisibility. The propagation of ferns was not understood: the seeds themselves were thought to be invisible and therefore possessed of the magic power of conferring invisibility.

46.   THE DEFINITION OF LOVE

This, one of Marvell's most intensely concentrated poems, is a highly individual variation on the Platonic conception of love. Plato held that the material world is no more than a flawed shadow of the ideal world. In the poem fate is represented as opposing, with an iron law, the realization of perfect love between man and woman, and for this reason the love between Marvell and his beloved, while it defies the laws of mathematics (lines 27–8), is, in its purely Platonic perfection, of cosmic proportions. Despite the ingenuity and the lack of concrete reference, this poem has the ring of passionate and deeply felt experience.

*l.*24.   *Planisphere:* either a projection of a sphere on to a plane surface, or, more probably, an astrolate.

48.   THE PICTURE OF LITTLE T.C. IN A PROSPECT OF FLOWERS

In this poem Marvell pays homage to a very young girl The identity of T.C. has not been positively established; M suggests that it was Theophila Cornewall who, at the probable date of composition, was between eight and ten years old. It displays Marvell's special capacity to breathe life, individuality and profound sense into a convention, in this case that of semi-pastoral, artificial compliment to a beauty. His wish that T.C. should withstand men until she is old enough to make the right choice is no mere formal tribute; and the fear that she may not live to maturity (death-rate among children in the 17th century was very high) adds a personal note. Typical of Marvell's handling of traditional material are his references to the flowers: they are natural imagery in the poem, but no 17th-century reader would miss the overtones from the folklore of flowers, by which the rose meant passion and the violet modesty, while on the other hand the tulip, being a comparatively recent (1578 from Turkey) importation, was simply the tulip.

*l.*17.   *in time:* before it is too late; *compound:* come to terms.

*l.*20.   *wheels:* The older T.C. is foreseen as driving a chariot of war over the hearts of her admirers.

*l.*22.   *but:* merely.

*l.*27.   *errours:* i.e. Nature has given the tulip no scent, the rose thorns and the violet too short a life.

*l.*36.   *Flora:* Goddess of flowers and fertility.

49.   TOM MAY'S DEATH

Thomas May, poet, historian and translator of Lucan's *Pharsalia* (1628), was born in 1595. He early gained the favour of Charles I, but changed his political allegiance in 1640—because, his detractors (probably rightly) charged, he had failed to obtain the post of Poet Laureate on the death of Ben Jonson in 1637. Aubrey says tersely: 'He stood candidate for the Laurell after B. Jonson; but Sir William Davenant carried it'. May published in 1647 his official history of the Long Parliament. His tragedies and original poems are said to be extravagantly bad. He died in his sleep in 1650—some said of suffocation because he had tied his night-cap too tight, others said of drink. His body was removed from Westminster Abbey and a monument to him pulled down in 1661. He was reputed to be a heavy drinker, a fact with which Marvell, who himself enjoyed his wine, makes great play. It has been suggested that lines 85–90 of this satire refer to the exhumation and that therefore it was written after the Restoration; but the passage can just as easily be interpreted as a protest that May, a poor poetaster and a timeserver, should have been accorded the honour of an Abbey burial. 1650, the year of May's death, is a much more likely date, for at this time Marvell was still largely Royalist in at least his personal sympathies. However, it is the facts of May's poor character and dubious motives that prompted this satire from Marvell. The poem is important as showing that Marvell, although capable of supreme detachment in his finest work, could also express powerful and direct indignation. The complaint here, however, is less political than literary. Lines 63–71 manifest an unfamiliar but significant side of Marvell's character: in a sense they justify his attitude of political detachment in the *Horatian Ode*. His express admiration of Jonson is noteworthy, and is a solid fact worth much more than biased conjectures about his political allegiances.

*l.*6.   *Stevens ally:* a street full of taverns where May may have lived, and where of course there were no trees or grass.

*l.*7.   *Popes head:* an inn in Lombard Street.

*l.*10.   *Ares:* Mars; possibly also the name of an innkeeper.

*l.*11.   *port:* bearing.

*l.*13.   *Ben:* Ben Jonson, the acknowledged mentor of all the younger poets.

*ll.*17–18.   a Dantesque image of destruction.

*l.*21.   *Emathian:* F reads 'Emilthian'; but May's translation of Lucan's *Pharsalia* begins 'Warres more than Civill on Aemathian plaines', so that Cooke's emendation is surely correct.

169

l.30. A line well worth noting by those who wish to understand Marvell.
l.38. An allusion to an old scandal: May had physically attacked the Lord Chamberlain, then the Earl of Pembroke, in 1633/4, after a masque performed at Court. Later the King pardoned him and gave him fifty pound pieces.
l.41. *Polydore:* Polydore Virgil (*c.* 1470–1555), an Italian who came to England and became Archdeacon of Wells and a historian; *Allan:* a Scuthian people, the Alani, mentioned in *Pharsalia*; they were held to resemble the Vandals ('Vandole') and Goths.
l.44. May's *History of the Long Parliament* is sickeningly full of classical parallels.
l.50. The Virgin Mary's house was supposed to have been miraculously conveyed to Loretto.
l.54. May wrote a continuation of Lucan.
l.62. *Basket Guelphs and Gibellines:* M thinks 'Basket' is an allusion to the *borsa* or bag which received votes in the Florentine elections. The Guelphs and Ghibellines were two opposed Florentine factions, perpetually fighting one another.
l.74. *Spartacus:* leader of the slaves' rebellion against the Romans in the 1st century B.C.; this may refer to Essex or even to Fairfax: May at various times praised both.
l.90. *Phlegeton:* a flaming river in Hades.
l.91. *Cerberus:* watchdog at the gates of Hades.
l.92. *Megaera:* one of the Furies, usually represented as winged women with snaky locks.
l.93. *Ixion:* suffered in Hades by being bound on a perpetually turning wheel.

52. THE MATCH

This somewhat contrived, highly 'metaphysical' poem is Marvell at his neatest but least compelling. Nature stores up against her old age a distillation of all beauty, which becomes Celia; Love stores up all his power for warmth and aggression, which by spontaneous combustion becomes the writer of the poem.

54. THE MOWER AGAINST GARDENS

In this and the three poems that follow 'the Mower is a special variant of the stock Swain, more English and also more of a person. Sometimes he is a simple countryman, and sometimes his simplicity is the last reward of sophistication' (B & LT). He is, however, other things besides: in his original state he is the natural man warring against the sophistication represented by formal gardening and courtly artifice in love. We must beware of identifying him with Marvell himself, the author of *The Garden*. Like love itself, the Mower is both destroyer and victim. There is a further reason why Marvell makes his 'Swain' a mower, rather than, for instance, a shepherd. Indeed, he specifically rejects the conventional pastoral figure of the lover as shepherd (*Damon the Mower*, 49–56). The Mower, with his sharp scythe, is a ravisher, at once a killer and a procreator, far removed from the Theocritean warbler of love-plaints: he is active. There is ample evidence that Marvell and his contemporaries were fully aware of the *lingua franca* of English folklore with its agricultural metaphors. The phallophoric significance of the plough and the scythe were part of the stock-in-trade of popular song. The application of 'mowing' to sexuality in action is quite specific (see J. Reeves, *The Everlasting Circle*, pp. 21–33 *passim*).

What is Marvell saying in these strange and highly original poems? He is profoundly disturbed by the conflict in his own mind between wild, natural sexuality and the demands of society as represented by woman, whose self-withdrawal, however destructive it may be of man's peace of mind, is the essential preserver of civilized human continuity. In this series, in fact, Marvell is making a vital and permanently valid poetic exploration of a central area of experience.

*ll.*1–2.   Man, being evil, corrupted Nature. In the succeeding lines Marvell goes on, with matchless irony, to describe how Nature itself is corrupt. *Luxurious:* voluptuous; lustful.

*ll.*5–6.   Even the air is regarded as tainted because instead of being free it is now enclosed; the reference is of course to formal gardening.

*l.*7.   The reference is to manure.

*l.*9.   *double:* a pun: deceitful; and referring to the pink, which by cultivation and manuring becomes a double bloom.

*ll.*13–16.   Tulips were especially fashionable—in fact became a 'mania'—in the 1630's.

*l.*18.   *Marvel of Peru:* an exotic importation from the West Indies.

*ll.*29–30.   Refers to the practice of breeding fruit without pollination, which from the point of view of the 'natural' man represented by the Mower is immoral. The implied *stoneless* cherry puns on 'stones' in its meaning of 'testicles', a necessary adjunct of human procreation.

*l.*40.   *with us:* i.e. in the fields.

55.   DAMON THE MOWER. See headnote to THE MOWER AGAINST GARDENS

*l.*6.   *scorching:* July is Juliana's month.

*l.*12.   *hamstring'd:* crippled by the heat.

*l.*13.   *But:* only.

*l.*15.   *within:* i.e. remained in its hole.

*l.*18.   *Dog-star:* Sirius, which was supposed to produce heat.

*l.*21.   *mads:* This is the MS reading of a copy of F with MS corrections, in the Bodleian Library. It seems very much better than F's 'made', although the extent of the authenticity of the MS corrections is not certainly known.

l.22. Phaeton: son of Helios the Sun-God. He was destroyed when he borrowed his father's chariot.

l.38. hony due: an ideally sweet substance.

ll.57–8. 'I am not so bad looking, if I saw myself aright last time I used the crescent blade of my scythe as a mirror.'

l.83. Shepherds-purse . . . Clowns-all-heal: herbs traditionally used to treat wounds.

59. THE MOWER TO THE GLO-WORMS

l.12. foolish Fires: ignes fatui: will o' the wisps.

60. THE MOWER'S SONG

In this poem the mower sees himself as having once viewed Nature with a calm and untroubled mind. When he falls in love with Juliana, Nature suddenly appears even more beautiful. However, the meadows now seem deceitful, since they rejoice while he pines with grief: they show no compassion for the slighted lover. Therefore, matching Juliana's destructiveness with his own, he lays about him with his scythe, thus revenging himself on nature by bringing death to it. The sexual implications of this are obvious.

61. AMETAS AND THESTYLIS MAKING HAY-ROPES

l.12. then: than.

l.16. Hay: a pun: a hay was a dance of serpentine movement ending with the partners kissing each other.

62. MUSICKS EMPIRE

This poem is probably an elaborate compliment to Fairfax, 'the Conqueror' of the final stanza. More overtly, it is a typically ingenious allegorical account of the origin and development of music, of which Marvell was a devotee.

l.5. Jubal: 'the father of all such as handle the harp and organ' (*Genesis*, iv, 21).

l.6. tuned: Cooke F's 'tun'd' cannot possibly be made to scan; *Jubilee:* used here in the sense of 'release'.

l.8. Organs City: a metaphor suggested by the appearance of an organ.

l.23. Fairfax had retired.

63. THE GARDEN

Whether or not it is right to regard this most famous of all Marvell's poems as the product of a Puritan mind, it certainly could not have been written at any other time. But this is no narrow, homiletic or didactic kind of Puritanism;

it may even be more accurate to regard it as primarily Platonic in the most obvious sense: the pleasures of ambition and society are rejected because they are imperfect, corrupt, mere shadows of the real. The ambitious athlete, soldier or poet wins only a garland from a single tree; in Marvell's garden all flowers and trees are present, and there is repose from the 'uncessant Labours' of the ambitious.

But, although its affinities with the Garden of Eden are explored, Marvell's garden is not Paradise before the Fall. Rather it is an ideal testing-place or place of residence for the soul in its quest for innocence and perfection. Therefore he writes, 'Your sacred plants, if here below/Only among the Plants will grow'.

The lust engendered by the white and red of beautiful women is here transmuted into love by 'this lovely green'. Such lovers as wander here, made cruel by their desire, cut their mistress' names in the bark of the trees; Marvell only cuts in them the names of the trees themselves. Desire for beauty, he implies, abuses beauty: thus Apollo hunted Daphne, not for lust, but only that she might turn into a laurel, Pan Syrinx only that she might become a reed. However, even the sensual pleasures of the garden are snares. The mind rejects even the pleasures of Nature in favour of those of joy and contemplation, by which alone it may achieve the imaginative state—creating 'Far other Worlds and Seas'. This is not to be confused with a misanthropic withdrawal from the world: only in this way can life be lived fully. (Those interested might compare this with the French novelist Alain Robbe-Grillet's 'behaviourist' view of objects, and his attack on the anthropomorphism of literature.)

The above is offered, not as a paraphrase but as a general guide to the thought of the poem. It would be wrong to assume that Marvell intended to make a series of didactic statements. He is clearly ambivalent in his attitude to a number of facets of experience. Thus the paradox that man corrupts nature by trying to perfect or improve it, as in delightful gardens, haunts his poetry (see lines 39-40), but is never really resolved. Marvell's 'solution' of the problem is, perhaps, that there is no solution other than passive acceptance.

Subtle and many-layered though *The Garden* is, it is worth recalling that Marvell must certainly have had in mind, as he wrote it, Fairfax's garden.

l.2. the Palm, the Oke, or Bayes: awarded respectively to athletes, soldiers and poets.

l.23. your: Cooke you F.

ll.29-33. One of Marvell's profoundest paradoxes. For does not the lover, in the frenzy of his desire, truly seek the repose offered by Nature?

l.37. curious: exquisite, but also used here to mean 'cultivated'.

ll.39-40. These lines re-enact the Fall, subtly recalling the saying 'All flesh is grass'. Both 'grass' and 'grace' were pronounced similarly in the 17th century.

*ll.*47–8. A true example of ambiguity. This can mean either 'reducing every-thing material to nothing material', i.e. transforming matter into spirit; or 'holding the material world as of no worth compared to a green thought in a green shade'. The two meanings are not incompatible: the latter may lead to the former. Imagination 'annihilates' the physical world. The creative prin-ciple (i.e. greenness) is, in a sense that Platonism easily explains, superior to what it creates in mere physical form. True physical ecstasy reaches beyond the physical.

*l.*54. *whets:* preens its plumage with its beak.

*ll.*71–2. Time itself could not exist without the actions of Nature.

66. FLECKNO, AN ENGLISH PRIEST AT ROME

Richard Flecknoe (died 1678), Irish Roman Catholic priest and minor writer, was pilloried by both Dryden (*Mac Flecknoe*, 1682) and Marvell. He visited the English College at Rome 1645–7, and it is therefore likely that this satire, whose casual, rumbustious tone in some ways recalls Donne, was written before 1650. It may be inferred that Flecknoe was somewhat grotesque, a bad poet and a bore. M suggests that Marvell became acquainted with Flecknoe while acting as tutor to Edward Skinner. The satiric technique of the conversation with the priest was later used by Marvell in parts of *The Rehearsall Transpros'd*.

*l.*3. *Melchizedeck:* King of Salem and Priest of the most high God (*Genesis*, xiv, 18).

*l.*4. *My Lord Brooke:* Fulke Greville. Apparently Flecknoe claimed a con-nection with him.

*ll.*11–17. There are a number of rather tedious puns here, pointing to the coffin-life properties of Flecknoe's room. *Seav'n:* refers to the river; *Seeling* meant wall-hangings and wainscot; *Sheet* puns on bed-sheet and winding-sheet; a Stanza (later Flecknoe is represented as dressing himself in stanzas of his own composition) means a room in Italian, and an *Appartement* is a suite of rooms.

*l.*21. *exercise:* exorcise.

*l.*65. *stich:* (1) a stitch in sewing, (2) grimace.

*l.*74. *Sotana:* cassock.

*ll.*96–104. These lines satirise some nice points of natural philosophy, e.g. *penetration* refers to an absurd dispute about whether two bodies could occupy the same space at the same time, cf. *Horatian Ode*, p. 119, 42.

*l.*104. *By* Cooke *But* F.

*l.*98. *Delightful:* delighted.

*ll.*125–6. According to Suetonius, Nero made it illegal for anyone to leave his presence while he was reciting his own verses.

ll.127–8. In mythology the pelican feeds its young with the flesh and blood of its own breast.

l.130. foul copies: rough drafts.

l.133. pilled: peeled.

l.137. Chancres: syphilitic sores; *Poulains:* sores in the groin, probably of venereal origin.

l.152. The Greek tyrant Phalaris ordered the sculptor Perillus to make a brazen bull, in which he intended to burn his enemies alive. The first victim was Perillus.

l.158. 'Twas: Grosart + *was* F.

71. TO HIS WORTHY FRIEND DOCTOR WITTY UPON HIS TRANSLATION OF THE POPULAR ERRORS

Dr. Robert Witty, a Hull physician known to Marvell, translated into English a Latin work, *Popular Errors . . . In Physick,* by his fellow physician, also of Hull, James Primrose. This poem, signed 'Andrew Marvell', together with its Latin companion, was printed in the book, which was published in 1651, and afterwards in F. This text follows F, except in line 30, as noted. Lines 4–16 embody a common-sense theory of translation, which clearly transcends the somewhat trivial occasion of the poem. In a letter of 2 April 1667 to Lord Wharton, discussing a poem by Simon Ford on the burning of London, Marvell wrote: 'The Latin . . . hath severall excellent heights, but the English translation is not so good; and both of them strain for wit and conceit more then becomes the gravity of the author of the sadnesse of the subject'.

ll.1–2. 'The translation has to make way for the commendatory verses'—M.

l.4. Cypress vail: black linen veil.

l.17. Cælia: As M says, citing *Upon Appleton House, ll.*707/8. This probably refers to Mary Fairfax, and is further evidence 'that Marvell's residence in the Fairfax household dates from the winter of 1650–1'.

l.30. Cawdles: 1651; *Cawdles:* F thin gruel, often fed to the sick; *Almondmilk:* a preparation of sweet blanched almonds and water, still used as a handlotion.

72. ON MR. MILTON'S PARADISE LOST

This poem was first printed, signed 'A.M.', at the beginning of the second edition of *Paradise Lost* (1674). This text follows F except in lines 33 and 45, as noted. Marvell had in the previous year written a defence of Milton in *The Rehearsall Transpros'd.* This tribute is evidence of his high personal regard and warm affection for Milton.

l.9. Sampson: The reference is to *Samson Agonistes,* which had appeared three years earlier, together with *Paradise Regained.*

l.18. *some less skilful hand:* Probably a reference to Dryden, then Poet
Laureate, with whom Marvell was on bad terms. Aubrey tells of how Dryden
applied to Milton for permission to put *Paradise Lost* into rhyme, and of how
'Mr Milton received him civilly, and told him he would give him leave to
tagge his verses'—for 'tag' see line 50.

l.30. *detect:* expose.

l.33. *treatst:* 1674 *treats* F.

ll.39–40. A reference to the belief that Birds of Paradise had no feet, and
therefore spent their lives in the air, on Wing.

l.45. *mightst:* 1674 *might* F.

l.47. *Town-Bays:* Dryden. The common nickname 'Bays' for Dryden
originated in the Court-wit Buckingham's *The Rehearsal* (1672). Dryden
attacked Marvell in the preface to *Religio Laici* (1682), as a 'Presbyterian
scribbler who sanctified libels and scurrility to the use of the good old cause'.
spells: M thinks this means '"does things by spells or stages", each rhymed
unit being a spell'; Macdonald says 'I don't know what this means'. We think
it means either 'exerts the magic spell of rhyme' or 'spells out the ends of his
lines so that they rhyme, as "spells" jingles with "Bells"'; in any case, Marvell
glances at what Milton called rhyme in the preface to *Paradise Lost*—'the
invention of a barbarous age'. Milton is said to have called Dryden 'a great
rhymer but no poet'. Marvell, who himself must be described as a rhymer
in the strictly technical sense, is here being deferential; possibly he no longer
regarded himself as a senior poet.

l.49. *bushy Points:* tasselled laces for fastening hose.

74. SENEC. TRAGED. EX THYESTE CHOR. 2

A translation from one of the choruses in a tragedy by the Latin playwright
Seneca.

75. UPON THE HILL AND GROVE AT BILL-BOROW

For Marvell's connection with Nun Appleton, Fairfax's country seat, see
Introduction, pp. 5–8. Bilbrough is five miles from Appleton House, the
subject of the succeeding poem. L writes aptly of both poems: 'They are
essentially private poems, almost . . . private jokes, intended only for the eye
of Marvell's friend and patron the Lord General, to whose so well attested
modesty the deliberately exaggerated and hyperbolical compliments must
have caused much amusement'. Fairfax himself wrote verse, and there is no
reason to suppose that because this was not very good he therefore lacked an
understanding of poetry. As L says, 'No doubt he admired in these two poems
a degree both of wit and of poetry which he himself could never hope to
achieve'. The Bilbrough poem is in parts half-playful, but perfectly realized.
The poem on Appleton House, easily Marvell's longest, is in one sense patch-

work, a series of short poems connected by a simple narrative device; but it does contain some of Marvell's most beautiful lines and passages, and is of great interest because it reveals certain things about its author that would not otherwise be known. Essentially it was written to delight and praise Fairfax, for whose character Marvell had the highest regard; it is also a virtuoso performance, calculated to surprise Marvell's patron with the power of his ingenuity and the delicacy of his feeling. The poem is as sardonically and cunningly non-Puritan as it is apparently Puritan, as demonstrated in our notes. It is known from the *Horatian Ode* that Marvell, reluctantly recognizing the necessity of making impossible decisions, had resolved to go along with the Cromwellian side; but residence with a cultivated parliamentarian general who had refused to become involved with the execution of the King and, as a moderate, had retired from active service ('For he did, with his utmost skill/ *Ambition* weed, but *Conscience* till') was what exactly suited Marvell's state of mind at the time. The shifting tone and sophistication of the poem reflects this satisfaction.

ll.1–8.   The perfection of the hill might serve as the model by which the world was made. These lines are perhaps the most perfect expression in English poetry of the way the beauty of a landscape can arouse feelings of the holiness of nature. Note the pun on 'Brow', suggesting the art of portraiture.

l.9.   *more unjust:* i.e. grander and less gentle landscape.

l.12.   *fright:* Cooke + frght F.

l.22.   *it:* Cooke + iv F.

l.27.   *farther:* Cooke further Grosart + furthe F.

ll.29–30.   Marvell makes the trees (line 35) on Bilbrough a landmark for sailors; but M doubts this and thinks that the notion, later recorded by other writers, may have its source in the fancy of this poem.

l.34.   *Plump:* M + Plum F. Plume Cooke 'Plump', meaning 'cluster', is clearly the correct reading.

l.43.   *Vera:* Anne, daughter of Sir Horace Vere and wife of Lord Fairfax.

l.56.   This refers to Fairfax.

l.73.   *ye:* Grosart + the F. The MS symbol for *y* and *th* were identical; a confusion which has led to 'Ye olde teashoppe' fantasy and so on.

78.   UPON APPLETON HOUSE, TO MY LORD FAIRFAX

For a discussion of this poem, and its structure, see pp. 5–8 Nun Appleton House was begun about 1637, the year of Fairfax's marriage to Anne Vere, and finished in 1650.

ll.5–6.   The architect's own brain, extended by the ambitiousness of his project, becomes a model for it.

l.8.   *arch the Brows:* i.e. in amazement; note the typically ingenious pun on 'arch'.

l.22.   *Mole:* Cooke Mose F. M has 'Mote'; but earlier editors' (Cooke and Aitken) 'Mole' is surely more Marvellian in its combined senses of i. the mole (the mammal) as blind builder, ii. massive stone structure.

l.24.   *the first Builders:* who built the Tower of Babel; hence the thought of the next line.

l.29.   *larger sized Men:* it was popularly believed that man had become progressively smaller throughout the ages.

l.30.   *loop:* loophole.

l.40.   Marvell compares Romulus' traditional dwelling with a beehive, and not too seriously suggests that, unlike Fairfax in the large Nun Appleton, he fitted it as compactly as a bee.

l.42.   *Lines:* of the house, and of this poem; this kind of pun, with the playful 'admirable', demonstrates just how private and particular the occasion of this poem was.

l.46.   A reference to the insoluble mathematical problem of 'squaring the circle', which was much discussed and attempted in the 17th century. Hobbes was convinced that he had found a solution, but he was mistaken. The problem was to devise a formula by which the area of a circle, πr^2, could be expressed as a square.

ll.51–2.   Another ingenious joke. The roof of the hall was spherical; Fairfax's greatness, as he comes, is supposed to have made it so.

l.65.   *Frontispiece of Poor:* 'Frontispiece' means 'decorated entrance'. Presumably the subject of the decoration was a rich man giving largesse to the poor: Fairfax is said to have been conscientious in this respect.

l.71.   Fairfax himself wrote some lines about his house. They begin:

> Thinke not ô Man that dwells herein
> This House's a stay but as an Inne.

l.73.   *Bishops-hill:* (where Mary Fairfax was born) and Denton were houses which came into the Fairfax family as part of the estate of Isabel Thwaites, whose story is told in the succeeding stanzas. Early in the 16th century this heiress was wooed by Fairfax's ancestor, William Fairfax; but her guardian, Lady Anna Langton, Prioress of Nun Appleton, shut her up. Eventually she was released by force; and she married William Fairfax.

ll.97–224.   This long description of the nunnery is, as has been pointed out, distinctly uncharacteristic of contemporary Puritan attitudes. The point is that in this story the reader easily and naturally assumes that Lady Anna Langton and the nuns are villainous and that Fairfax is virtuous. But this reflects no more than a superficially conventional view. Actually Marvell, by making both the nunnery and Lady Anna's sensuality appealing, achieves a remarkable and subtle balance. As MCB & GLT write, 'her [Lady Anna's] epicureanism, though meant to be reprehensible, is too strong to be rejected completely. Like her abbey, it becomes the foundation of the later structure'. Critics who assume that Marvell was a committed Puritan considerably oversimplify the issue: he was, rather, a man who did not reject Puritanism out of hand (as comic, evil, or horrifying), a man who assimilated its best features into the highly civilized and sophisticated structure of his own thought and behaviour.

*l.*105.   *Armour white:* 'The Cistercian habit is white'—M.

*ll.*107-8.   See Matthew xxv, 1-13.

*l.*139.   *Man:* Cooke + Mant F.

*ll.*169-76.   This stanza, by its irony ('yet so nice') and wise beauty, shows a marked—although oblique—disapproval of conventional Puritan harshness and neurotic rejection of 'Delight'.

*ll.*239-40.   It is difficult to think that Fairfax and Marvell, as the latter came to this point in his reading of the poem to his patron, did not laugh. We ignore both the essentially private nature of the poem, and its high good spirits, at our peril: to read it in too purely 'literary' a light is a serious error.

*l.*241.   The son of William and Isabel Fairfax, Sir Thomas, fought in Europe; his son, also Thomas, was knighted for gallantry.

*l.*281.   *Heroe:* The hero is almost certainly Lord Fairfax himself, rather than any of his forbears.

*l.*301.   *the Virgin Nymph:* Mary Fairfax.

*l.*323.   *Paradise:* Cooke + *Paradise* F.

*ll.*349-50.   Fairfax had been responsible for the defence of the Cinque Ports. See ll. 285-289.

*l.*351.   *spann'd:* limited.

*l.*370.   *unfathomable Grass:* This phrase, in which 'unfathomable' is played upon in its senses of 'bottomless' and 'incomprehensible', and at the same time applied to the grass rather than the sea, is quintessential Marvell. Cf. note on *ll.*39-40 of *The Garden.*

*l.*389.   *Israelites:* M; Israelites Cooke Israaliies F.

*l.*395.   *Rail:* corncrake.

*l.*402.   *Cates:* provisions.

*l.*416.   *Sourdine:* trumpet.

*l.*426.   *Hay:* The hay was a dance, cf. Shepherds hay.

*l.*428.   *Alexanders sweat:* Plutarch says this was sweet-smelling.

*l.*439.   *Roman Camps:* actually refers to the tumuli of an earlier, British race.

*l.*444.   *Lilly:* Sir Peter Lely, the painter, who is here fancied as painting on stretched cloth.

*l.*447.   *Toril:* bull-ring.

*l.*450.   *Levellers:* a communistic party formed by Winstanley after the Civil War.

*l.*454.   *Beast:* Cooke Breast F.

*l.*456.   William Davenant, the poet, wrote an unfinished epic, *Gondibert* (1652), in which the line 'strait an universal Herd appears' refers to the sixth day of the Creation of the World.

*l.*462. *Multiplying:* Multiplying F.

*l.*464. *Constellations:* Constellations F.

*l*472. *astonish'd:* astonish F.

*ll.*475–6. Marvell wittily adapts the legend that horse's hair turns into eels if put into water; leeches can attach themselves to horses while they are drinking.

*ll.*489–92. The Vere and Fairfax families are joined into one as two different woods can be spliced together; Marvell extends the reference to Noah, 'the first Carpenter' (line 485).

*l.*502. *a Fifth Element:* i.e. one beyond the familiar ones of earth, fire, air and water.

*l.*535. An allusion to the folk-belief that the stork was in the habit of leaving behind one of her young for the owner of the house in which she had made her nest.

*l.*537. *Hewel's:* woodpecker's.

*l.*538. *Holt-felsters:* woodcutters.

*ll.*555–6. One of Marvell's wisest observations: human beings have a thirst for 'sin'. The implication is that they invented sin because it is forbidden. This is far in advance of most contemporary Puritan thinking. The parenthesis is not closed in F.

*l.*562. *Birds:* Btrds F.

*l.*577. The Cumaean Sybil wrote her prophecies on leaves.

*l.*580. *Mexique Paintings:* The Mexicans made pictures by gumming together the coloured plumage of birds.

*l.*586. *Mask:* masque-costume.

*l.*591. *antick Cope:* a phrase borrowed from Milton. The vault of branches overhead is both antic and antique.

*ll.*598–600. The winds winnow the chaff from the grain in both his hair and his thoughts; *shed:* separate; part.

*l.*610. *gadding Vines:* Another phrase from Milton, this time from Lycidas (published at Cambridge, 1638, during Marvell's time there).

*l.*636. *slick:* sleek.

*l.*649. *Quills:* floats.

*l.*651. *young Maria:* Mary Fairfax, then thirteen.

*l.*660. *Bonne:* a disyllable.

*l.*668. *Shuts:* shutters.

*l.*669. *modest Halcyon:* the kingfisher, modest because seldom seen.

*l.*673. *She:* the kingfisher, to whom Marvell is comparing Mary Fairfax in a long metaphor.

*ll.*733–4. 'Your own face will still mock, in the mirror, your efforts to keep it beautiful, through your bad complexion, which is like a mask.' *Black-bag:* mask.

l.753.   *Thessalian Tempe's Seat:* a beautiful valley between Olympus and Ossa.

l.755.   *Aranjuez:* Aranjuez, beautiful gardens near Madrid.

l.756.   *Bel-Retiro:* a palace near Madrid.

l.770.   *Leathern Boats:* coracles.

ll.771–2.   Marvell faintly mocks the hyperbolic intensity of the penultimate stanza by indulging in a characteristic joke.

l.776.   *them;* the coracles.

106.   ON THE VICTORY OBTAINED BY BLAKE OVER THE SPANIARDS
IN THE BAY OF SANTACRUZ IN THE ISLAND OF TENERIFF
1657

As a native of Hull, Marvell was interested in naval affairs. A version of this poem was printed, during his lifetime, in 1674 in *A New Collection of Poems and Songs;* the same book was reprinted in 1678 as *Melpomene.* But, as M points out, the original version, which did not appear until the 1681 Folio, was addressed to Cromwell (see especially lines 16, 'your flags', and 145–8). All traces of this were cut out of the 1674 version. We reprint F. England declared war on Spain in 1655. On 20 April 1657 Admiral Blake, who for nearly two years had been blockading the Spanish coast in wait for her treasure ships returning from America, destroyed a fleet of sixteen at Teneriffe without the loss of a single one of his own vessels. There was great public rejoicing. Blake was ordered home, but died on 7 August 1657, two hours before he reached Plymouth. Marvell's poem was therefore written between late April and early August of that year (not in 1653, as stated by B & LT). This is one of Marvell's public poems, written at a time when Cromwell had his political support. Blake acts throughout as an appropriate symbol for Cromwell himself, who must have disappointed Marvell by refusing the offer of the crown on 8 May, twenty days before news of Blake's victory reached England. The Canary Isles, against which the Spanish fleet descends, stand for England, against which the Spanish Armada had descended in 1588. This poem should be read in close conjunction with *The First Anniversary . . .,* which preceded it. See our notes on this poem, pp. 186–188.

l.3.   *swoome:* swam, here meaning float.

l.4.   *Guilt:* puns on gilt.

l.9.   *Intrails:* Intails F.

ll.24–38.   An account of the Canary Isles, but at the same time of England as it might be if Cromwell accepted the crown (see lines 39–44).

l.59.   *Oar:* over.

l.117.   *Stainer:* Sir Richard Stayner, one of Blake's subordinates.

l.129.   *never . . . a Spire:* Ne'r . . . aspire 1674 and modern eds.

*l.*145. *your:* Cromwell's.

*l.*149. *Sconce:* defence.

*ll.*159–60. The reference is to the English Civil War as well as to the war with Spain.

III. A DIALOGUE BETWEEN THYRSIS AND DORINDA

This, which is one of Marvell's least important poems, is the most textually corrupt of all those in F, its position in which (between *On the Victory Gained by Blake . . .* and *The First Anniversary*) is clearly wrong. M constructed a better text with the aid of versions he discovered in MS books. It was set to music more than once. We have printed the F version, incorporating some, although not all, of M's emendations; but we have made no distinction between the various MSS.

*l.*3. *Thyrsis:* MS Thrisis F.

*ll.*7–8. MS *I know no way, but one, our home*
           Is our Elizium? F.

*l.*14. *fly?:* MS fly. F.

*l.*20. *away?:* MS away F.

*l.*25. *No . . . there thine Ears:* MS And there most sweetly thine Ear F.

*l.*26. *Spheres:* MS Sphere F.

*l.*27. *Oh sweet! oh sweet!:* MS, omitted in F.

*l.*28. *Antidate:* antedate.

*l.*29. *to:* MS, omitted in F.

*l.*33. *sing Consorts:* singing in harmony.

*l.*34. *Cool:* MS, *Cold* F.

*l.*41. *Convinc':* MS, *Convinc't* F.

*l.*42. *adieu: adiev* F.

*l.*43. F omits Thyrsis.

*ll.*45/4. F gives these lines to Dorinda, but the Chorus of the MSS seems much more likely.

*l.*45. *Carillo:* MS Corellia F.

113. THE CHARACTER OF HOLLAND

War with Holland broke out in May 1652; and Deane (l. 150) was killed in action in June 1653. This poem was therefore written some time between these dates, probably just after the English victory over the Dutch off Portland in February 1653. Some lines from it appeared in 1665, with a conclusion apparently not by Marvell; the complete version first appeared in F. Rivalry with Holland was common to both Commonwealth and Restoration England. This is one of Marvell's crudest satires. Possibly Professor Frank

Kermode had it in mind, together with some of the later popular satires, when he described Marvell as a 'chauvinist'. However, such a description is unfair, even though Marvell was capable of adopting a chauvinistic pose for satirical purposes. Within ten years Marvell's attitude to Holland had become more reasonable, as his satire *Last Instructions to a Painter* demonstrates. Here his tone is deliberately unreasonable: he is not even pretending to try to be fair or balanced. Even at its best the satire reaches only a brilliant undergraduate level. It should not be considered as one of Marvell's serious poems, bur rather as the product of a mood.

l.5. *alluvion:* deposit of matter by flood, and therefore a legal term for the formation of new land by the action of water.

l.8. A sneer at the allegedly heavy drinking habits of the Dutch.

l.28. *Level-coyl: lever le cul,* a game in which the players struggle to unseat one another and seat themselves in turn.

l.32. *Cabillau:* cod.

l.49. *Dyke-grave:* officer in charge of the dykes.

l.53. *Half-anders:* a pun on Hollanders, in keeping with the boisterous tone of the rest of the poem

l.62. *Poor-John:* dried hake.

ll.65–6. *Marg'ret:* a legendary woman of the Hague who was supposed to have had three hundred and sixty-five children at one birth. *Hans-in-Kelder:* Jack-in-the-cellar, thus, child in the womb. *Hans-Town:* member of the Hanseatic league.

l.78. *Village:* Because the Hague was denied a voice in the Assembly of Estates, it was described as 'the largest village in Europe'.

l.80. *Hogs: Hoog-mogenden,* high and mighty, was the official title of the States-General. *Bores:* a pun on Boers.

l.88. *a:* omitted in F.

l.94. Dutchmen were called butter-boxes.

l.96. *Snick and Sneer:* cut and thrust (with knives).

ll.117–118. The Dutch were said to have attacked Blake's fleet while negotiating for a treaty.

l.127. *careen:* heel over.

l.130. There was supposed to be a fortnight's calm while the legendary halcyon brooded on her nest.

l.135. *Bucentore:* the State barge of the Venetian republic.

ll.137–8. Almost certainly an allusion to the recent English naval victory off Portland; *now:* Thompson + now F.

118. AN HORATIAN ODE UPON CROMWELL'S RETURN FROM
     IRELAND

In all but two of the known copies of Marvell's 1681 folio this poem was cancelled, doubtless because the publisher felt that it seemed much too sympathetic towards the killer of the reigning king's father. Marvell must have written it about midsummer 1650, not long before he took up his tutorial post at Nun Appleton. Fairfax resigned his appointment as commander-in-chief because he did not wish to take part in a campaign against Scotland unless the Scots invaded England. Cromwell, who returned from his savagely successful Irish campaign at the end of May, took Fairfax's place; on 22 July 1650 he entered Scotland. M notes that the suggestion of some critics, that this ode represents Fairfax's view of the political situation, is not supported by any evidence that Marvell knew his future employer at this time. Besides, the poem very obviously represents Marvell's own painfully reached view—although it is clear, from it, that he found Fairfax's position a sympathetic one. We know of no other political poem (outside the drama) of such power and profundity as this. Its detachment is, as has often been remarked, almost superhuman. But it is not 'cold': the balance Marvell achieves provides an object lesson. The metre is his own invention. The greatness of the poem consists in the manner in which it deliberately transcends the personal opinions and prejudices of its author. Commentators forget (curiously) that Marvell was a poet, and understand the opening lines to be a simple statement that, in the words of one of them, 'study and the arts' are 'inappropriate to such crucial times'. This is seriously to misunderstand Marvell. When we realize that he was himself a poet, the note of irony is unmistakable; but it is not an irony that is intended to diminish Cromwell, whom Marvell clearly considers to be a man of destiny. (What, as a poet, he thinks of men of destiny is, of course, another question.) In this poem Marvell is a constitutional monarchist —as he remained throughout his life. It is at least possible that while he admired and respected Cromwell, he never actually much liked him as a man; he did not admire, and he attacked, Charles II, whom, however, he much amused, and probably liked personally. It is to be noted that Marvell, in common with others who sympathized with Charles I, erroneously attributes (ll. 47–52) to Cromwell a cunning plot: that he deliberately induced Charles I to escape from Hampton Court in order to further his own political designs. Had Marvell been as wholehearted a supporter of Cromwell as many critics maintain, then he would not have mentioned this matter at all—it was after all a Royalist fiction. M, and others, naïvely insist that Marvell sees Cromwell as a man without political ambition; these lines prove the contrary. Whether or not he came to admire Cromwell more in the next few years, here he expresses some personal distaste for him: in the irony of the opening, the attribution of the 'plot', and in the line about the King's death, '*He* nothing common did or mean', with the undoubtedly ironic emphasis on the personal pronoun. However, this distaste remains strictly personal. Unquestionably, the poem regrets the execution of the King and sees it as a tragedy.

But it accepts the new situation realistically, although not without irony. Commentators' most common error has been their insistence that Marvell, at this time, was actively and personally enthusiastic about Cromwell. Actually, the only unequivocal warmth he here permits himself is on the subject of the King's noble bearing on the scaffold—this is in line with his generally monarchist position. So far as Cromwell is concerned, he does not question his political greatness (which has not, incidentally, been seriously doubted by any but Catholic pseudo-historians); but his ironic undertones continually question Cromwell's *personal* greatness. This irony amounts to a kind of poetic despair, a subtle answer to the question, 'How should we feel about a non-poetic man who is, in the present circumstances, the most effective national leader?' However, Marvell does appreciate and emphasize the conflict, in Cromwell himself, between ambition and the desire for a retired life. Our notes attempt to make more particular corrections to what we consider to be the majority of critics' misreading. This misreading is based on an odd failure to remember that Marvell was a poet before he was a politician—and never more so, one may add, than when he was writing poems. This ode is a poem, not a tract.

l.1.   *forward Youth:* the youth eager to get on; but this is ironic in tone— 'Don't write poems, but get on with the invasion of Scotland'. At the same time, Marvell bitterly acknowledges that some such activity as war will be salutary in the circumstances.

l.2.   *now:* i.e. when England is preparing to invade Scotland.

l.15.   *Side:* (1) party, (2) 'The lightning is conceived as tearing through the side of its own body the cloud'—M; *through* is a disyllable, pronounced 'thorough'.

ll.27-8.   The tone is undoubtedly grudging; nevertheless, it is fair.

ll.31-2.   The implication is not that Cromwell is unequivocally unambitious, but that he appears to be. His 'highest plot' was in fact, according to Marvell, that of becoming ruler of the country by inducing Charles's escape from Hampton.

l.32.   *Bergamot:* a kind of pear.

ll.34-6.   Again, this is by no means unambiguous praise of Cromwell, even if it recognizes his historical greatness.

ll.37-40.   Here Marvell equates Cromwell with 'Fate', and acknowledges the need for him because of men's weakness; in other words, he regards him as a necessary evil.

l.42.   *penetration:* The occupation of a space by two bodies simultaneously. The meaning is that there is no room for both Charles and Cromwell.

l.44.   *greater Spirits:* This is not devoid of irony; especially in view of the praise of Charles that follows.

l.46.   Cromwell was wounded at Marston Moor.

l.49. *subtile:* The original meaning of the word is 'fine, like a net'.

l.52. *case:* cage, with a pun on the older (Middle English) sense of 'plight'.

l.85. *Commons:* Thompson + *Common* F.

l.104. *clymacterick:* decisive.

l.105. *Pict:* Scot, with an insulting pun on the Latin pingere, to paint: hence 'Party-coloured'.

ll.119–20. Not wholly approving, but Marvell is realistic; the emphasis on *Arts* is ironic.

121. THE FIRST ANNIVERSARY OF THE GOVERNMENT UNDER O.C.

This poem, written for December 1654, was published in quarto in 1665, we may be reasonably sure at Marvell's own instigation. It was reprinted with no significant variation in F, but was, of course, cancelled along with the *Horatian Ode* and the *Poem on the Death of O.C.*; like the other two poems, it survives in the British Museum copy. If it is not as wholly successful, as poetry, as the non-political poems Marvell wrote while employed by Fairfax, it is nevertheless of great subtlety and, above all, irony. The submissively eulogistic tone towards Cromwell must not be taken as reflecting Marvell's private attitude. But nor must it be misunderstood as straightforwardly ironic disapproval: it is a highly intelligent, subtle—perhaps over-subtle—poem. John M. Wallace has called it a 'deliberative' rather than a eulogistic poem. The point is that Cromwell, against all the odds, had proved a successful ruler; if he was a usurper, then Providence would put that right in due course. Marvell's admiration for him is rhetorical, with a rueful sidelong look at the true nature of rhetoric; it is also pragmatic, with a poetically wistful look at the nature of pragmatism. Since Cromwell had killed the King, there is also a certain irony in the fact that—as Marvell saw it—his situation was still an essentially royalist one. For Marvell now had a living to earn; his days of retirement were over. Chiefly, however, this poem is remarkable for the ironic and bitter distinction it brilliantly makes between political and human greatness. This distinction may never be more than implied; but it is there.

ll.1–12. The irony, unmistakably expressed in the sense of 'Cromwell is different from other mortals', is tempered by admiration for an energetic and, in the circumstances, incredibly successful politician whose pragmatism (Marvell recognized) was perpetually modified by a religious conscience. *l*.8 hints that Cromwell should become King.

l.12. An allusion to Cromwell's crest.

ll.13–48. These lines are an unequivocal exhortation to Cromwell to accept the crown. They contain a warning (*l*. 22) against attempting to accomplish too much; and they are notable for the manner in which they contrast personal coldness towards Cromwell with political admiration for him.

l.20. *China clay:* was believed to mature in the earth for one hundred years.

*l.*23.   *some one* (singular).

*l.*41.   *an:* 1655 and F.

*ll.*47–8.   An allusion, surely not in the least 'difficult', as Hugh Macdonald calls it, to the belief that men's souls would 'sound in perfect unison with the cosmos' were there not 'a corporeal barrier'; 'the function of music', which Cromwell loved, 'is to overcome this barrier'.

*ll.*49–86.   Contemporary allusions to Cromwell's love of music were mainly satirical (and not unreasonably so), and so, partly, is this. Amphion, son of Zeus, was said to have built a wall by his magical playing of the lute.

*l.*68.   *Instrument:* The Protectorate had been established in the previous year by the Instrument of Government.

*l.*90.   *Contingation:* a framework of boards, as in a floor.

*l.*99.   This begins a passage (to 158) on the subject of Cromwell's abortive project to found a Protestant League; but there are also allusions to Millenarian hopes and references to biblical prophecies in *Daniel* and *Revelations*.

*ll.*116–30.   Ostensibly the reference is to those Continental kings who will not join Cromwell in his Protestant League; but there is certainly a deliberate reminiscence of Charles I, particularly in 'by Errour . . . misled', and, of course, in the by no means complimentary description of Cromwell as a remorseless huntsman from whom no 'throne' (including, perhaps, the one he may in future sit on, since 'the same arts that did gain/A power, must it maintain') is secure. Again, here we get the impression that Marvell is expressing admiration rather than love—political subservience rather than moral approval.

*l.*144.   The inescapable inference is that Marvell did not share the hopes of the Millenarians, however much he may have sympathized with their idealism. Since these are not the times, then this is not, after all, the man. The argument that he believed these *were* the times is not consistent with the warnings he issues at the beginning of the poem, about expecting one man to accomplish everything; see also lines 149–58. In this discrepancy between the political potential of Cromwell and England's state of unpreparedness to receive him may be seen a hint of Marvell's feelings about the Protector's human deficiencies; but these feelings are not developed. The passage (131–58) is a key one, and has provoked considerable controversy. In *Destiny his Choice* John M. Wallace argues that if grace has been denied Cromwell 'it must either be because the time of the millennial kingdom has not yet come' or because 'mankind . . . is frustrating God's wish to endow Cromwell with the grace necessary to finish His work'. This is to take Marvell's involvement with theologico-political controversy too seriously: to deny his poetic intelligence, even his sense of humour. While the tone of the passage does proper justice to the sincerity and even nobility of Puritan hopes and aspirations, its very ambiguity is a wry comment on the nature of politics. Cromwell possessed power, but he lacked grace (above all, a human capacity); Charles lacked 'power' in the Cromwellian sense, but we have seen from the *Horatian Ode* that Marvell did not deny him grace. Wallace's assertion that 'the first hundred and thirty lines of the poem should . . . be read as a statement of Cromwell's fitness for his vocation', that he was ready to be anointed with oil and assume kingship, is not incorrect: Marvell did, but on pragmatic rather than on religious grounds, believe that Cromwell should be elected King. But he did not share the millenarian hopes of some of the Puritans that a new Kingdom would become established; the exhortations to Cromwell to accept the Crown are critical.

*l.*175.   Cromwell escaped death when his coach overturned in Hyde Park in September 1654.

*l.*183.   *threed:* thread.

*ll.*215-20.   A reference to *Kings*, ii, 11-13, in which Elisha rends his clothes in two and mourns for Israel.

*l.*224.   *headstrong Peoples Charioteer:* Elishah. Marvell exhorts Cromwell to be the English people's Elijah. This and the following exhortations to Cromwell to accept the Crown are, as noted above, at least tinged with criticism: the implication is that Cromwell is perverse in not following out the line of his ambition; the 'private' Cromwell is—ironically—no longer a consideration.

*ll.*249-64.   Gideon (*Judges*, viii and ix) refused the headship that was offered to himself and his son, saying that the Lord should rule over the tribe. Clearly Marvell thought that Cromwell's parallel refusal was a politically inadequate gesture.

*l.*270.   *Corposants:* St. Elmo's fire: lights in the sky thought by early sailors to be angels' bodies.

*l.*293.   *Chammish issue:* 'Chammish' means 'like Ham'; the following lines satirize various fanatical sects that proliferated in England during the Protectorate.

*l.*297.   The Fifth Monarchists were a notable sect. They believed that the Second Coming was at hand.

*l.*298.   *Quake:* a pun on the Quakers, whose influence was then spreading.

*l.*305.   *Feake and Simpson:* imprisoned for preaching sedition against Cromwell in 1654.

*l.*310.   *Alcorand:* the Koran.

*l.*313.   *Munser's rest:* In 1534 the Anabaptists, an early Puritan sect, established 'the New Jerusalem' in Munster in Westphalia; they abolished marriage, established polygamy, did away with private property, etc. They were dispossessed in the following year. There is also a fortuitous pun on one of the founders of the Anabaptists, Thomas Münzes.

*l.*319.   The Adamites, another of the many sects, went naked.

*l.*366.   *Leaguers:* besieging forces.

129. TWO SONGS AT THE MARRIAGE OF THE LORD FAUCONBERG AND THE LADY MARY CROMWELL

Lord Fauconberg, a kinsman of Fairfax, married Mary, third daughter of the Protector on 19 November 1657 at Hampton Court.

l.30. Anchises: Robert Rich had married Cromwell's fourth daughter a week earlier.

134. A POEM ON THE DEATH OF O.C.

This, too, was cancelled from all known copies of F except the BM copy, which itself lacks lines 185–324. Our text follows the BM copy to line 184, and then substantially reprints Thompson's text, which is probably accurate. Cromwell died on 3 September 1658, his birthday. There is little or no personal feeling in the elegy, but much political respect.

l.22. humane: human.

l.30. Elizabeth Claypole, Cromwell's second daughter, died on 6 August 1658.

l.45. i.e. they know by sense and not by knowledge.

l.48. his growing: Thompson her growing F.

ll.53–4. 'Cromwell suffers in the suffering of his likeness Elizabeth'—M.

l.78. A reference to the practice of holding a mirror to a dying person's lips.

ll.112–32. There were violent thunderstorms on the day before Cromwell died.

l.121. lead: Grosart + dead F.

ll.189–90. Lt.-Col. Fenwick was killed at the siege of Dunkirk on a day of public prayer.

l.245. Francisca. Cromwell's youngest daughter.

ll.321–2. Richard Cromwell, son of Oliver, succeeded his father.

151. TO HIS NOBLE FRIEND MR. RICHARD LOVELACE, UPON HIS POEMS

This was published over Marvell's signature in 1649 as one of the commendatory poems in front of Lovelace's *Lucasta*. It does not appear in F.

l.12. Civicke crowne: A garland of oak leaves was awarded to one who saved a citizen's life in battle.

l.15. Caterpillar: state-official; anti-literary clerk.

l.21. Censorship had been strongly enforced since 1643.

l.28. Houses priviledge: i.e. freedom of speech.

ll.31–2. Lovelace was imprisoned for presenting to parliament a Kentish petition on behalf of King Charles I.

ll.33–50. Lovelace was reputed to be adored by women.

152. UPON THE DEATH OF LORD HASTINGS

This charming and beautifully accomplished elegy appeared in *Lacrymae Musatum* (1649), along with others on Hastings by Dryden, Herrick and Sir John Denham. It does not appear in F. Hastings, eldest son of the sixth Earl of Huntingdon, died of smallpox at the age of nineteen or twenty in June 1649.

*l.*12. *Remora:* A fish that attaches itself to ships and was supposed by the ancients to have the power of staying them in their course.

*ll.*17–18. *They . . . yeer:* In heaven they measure a man's time not by their own (solar) time but by earthly time.

*l.*40. Hastings' mother was still alive.

*l.*43. Hastings died on the eve of his proposed wedding-day.

*l.*48. *Mayern:* the famous physician to whose daughter Hastings was to be married.

*l.*49. *Chymist:* alchemist.

*l.*50. *leap:*burst.

154. AN ELEGY UPON THE DEATH OF MY LORD FRANCIS VILLERS

The unique manuscript text of this poem is a quarto of eight pages in the library of Worcester College, Oxford. It is unsigned, but George Clark (1660–1730), collector, scholar and M.P., wrote on it 'by Andrew Marvell'. His manuscript ascriptions have, writes Macdonald, 'generally turned out to be correct'; in this case perhaps the only objection to Marvell's authorship exists in the minds of those who cannot bring themselves to admit that he was at one time an ardent royalist. Villiers, posthumous son of the murdered Duke of Buckingham, was himself killed in a skirmish near Kingston-on-Thames on 7 July 1648.

*l.*61. *Fair Richmond:* Villiers' sister married the first Duke of Richmond.

*l.*69. *Chlora:* This may be Mary Kirke, the daughter of Aurelian Townsend.

158. From THE LOYAL SCOT [lines 15–74]

This passage occurs, with some variations, in another satire that is unquestionably by Marvell, *The Last Instructions to a Painter*. This text is probably Marvell's final, revised one. It recalls Marvell the poet in a remarkable manner. Archibald Douglas commanded a company of Lord George Douglas' Scottish regiment, which later became the Royal Scots. The Dutch burned the ship, *The Royal Oak*, of which Douglas was captain; he had received orders to defend it to the death, and finally he burned with her.

*l.*31. *birding:* mocking.

*l.*52. *sodred:* soldered.

*l.*61. *Oeta:* Hercules was burnt, voluntarily, on Mount Oeta. *Alcides:* Hercules.

160. From THE LOYAL SCOT [lines 178–85]

This delightful satire exists in manuscript in a Latin version. There is little doubt that it is Marvell's. Colonel Thomas Blood was deprived of land in Ireland at the Restoration, and in revenge attempted to steal the crown, sceptre and globe from the Tower of London on 9 May 1671. Blood disguised himself as a priest, and he and his three accomplices might have succeeded if they had not been disturbed by the return of the son of the keeper, Edwards, whom they had bound and stabbed (but not mortally). Charles II examined Blood and not only forgave him but also, characteristically, restored his lands.

INDEX OF TITLES AND FIRST LINES
OF POEMS